Volume 5: Governance and Leadership

Decisions Decisions   Large Print Edition

Haneefa Mateen

Copyright © 2024 by Haneefa Mateen

All rights reserved.

No portion of this book may be reproduced in any form without written permission from the publisher and author, except as permitted by U.S. copyright law.

Acknowledgment is gratefully given to the authors of the book, Physicians of the Heart: A Sufi View of the Ninety-Nine Names of Allah, for granting permission to use their explanations of the ninety-nine names of Allah, in this book. Copyright © 2011 by Wali Ali Meyer, Bilal Hyde, Faisal Muqaddam, Shabda Khan. Sufi Ruhaniat International.

Disclaimer: Brief historical events are only included to explain the main purpose of the book of showing how the use of divination may have changed the course of current events. Events mentioned in this book are based on information and official documents available to the public. Some media information may later be determined to not be true. However, the author has tried to be as accurate as possible. Reference to sources are listed in the back of the book if readers want more details. Some experiences and opinions are from the author's perspective and are not intended as medical advice

COPYRIGHT

or the use of any techniques as a form of treatment for physical, medical, psychiatric, mental health problems either directly or indirectly. In the event that you use any of the information in this book for yourself, which is your constitutional right, the author and publisher assumes no responsibility or liability whatsoever for readers or purchasers of this book.

Book Cover art: Haneefa Mateen

Contents

Introduction	1
PART ONE: THE PRESIDENCY	7
Chapter 1: Deciding Who to Vote For President	8
Chapter 2: Contested Election and Insurrection	15
Chapter 3: Anniversary of the Insurrection	22
Chapter 4: Investigation Begins	26
PART TWO: OTHER CHALLENGES OF THE BIDEN PRESIDENCY	48

Chapter 5: COVID-19 and the Economy	49
Chapter 6: Unalienable Rights	57
Chapter 7: President Biden's Second State of the Union Address	82
Chapter 8: World Peace	88
PART THREE: ANOTHER WORLD WAR?	105
Chapter 9: Russia Invasion of Ukraine	106
Chapter 10: Israel-Hamas War	111
Chapter 11: Other Cultures' Wisdom	123
Chapter 12: Israel and Gaza Religious Beliefs	136
Chapter 13: My Reflections	145

Chapter 14: President Biden's Plea to Israel	160
Chapter 15: United Nations' and Other International Organizations' Involvement	171
Chapter 16: Why Would the United States Continue Vetoing UN Resolutions?	184
Chapter 17: Congressional Pressure	223
Chapter 18: True Faith and Love	241
Chapter 19 Our Children	258
Books, Articles and Videos Mentioned in this Book	265
Author's Bio	281

Introduction

If you were President of the United States what would you do? How would you make the necessary major decisions that would not only affect you, but also your country and by extension the world? As a world leader, much is at stake with crisis after crisis. Frantically worried you are going to make the wrong decision, you have many sleepless nights.

How would citizens know who to vote for? How can citizens trust their leaders? What is a true democracy anyway? With the wars raging in Ukraine and then the Gaza and Israel region after the U.S. pulled troops out of Afghanistan, who's to blame and how do we solve wars? Follow along with this spiritual guidance review of President Biden's responses to crises and his ultimate major decisions. Did he make the right decisions?

"Insanity is doing the same thing over and over again and expecting different results." Albert Einstein.

Been there done that. Are you truly ready to initiate change for the better? Or would you keep repeating the same obsolete worn out traditions and loyalties, knowing that these are no longer useful and causes harm? Fear of change and what others will think may have had you hesitate or stopped you.

One way to know what needs to be changed and how to change

is to use indigenous methods of divination. Divination? Yes. Inquiring, using spiritual guidance to learn what's best beyond personal or popular media opinions, emotions, biases, arguments and motives. Sincerely inquiring what is best for everyone, including the planet.

Divination provides roadmaps very similar to a GPS that lets you know where the traffic congestion is and guides you through the detours. GPS gives alerts and warnings ahead of time. Divination also gives you alerts and can help you get back on the main road of the important task ahead of you. Sometimes we get stuck in traffic or a car accident anyway. Divination shows us how to get through the crises without making the situation worse.

Each of the previous four volumes of this book series, Decisions Decisions: Getting Answers to Life's Challenges, introduces different methods of divination that I used to obtain guidance and followed for improving my personal situations. These books were written as memoirs.

In Volume 5: Governance and Leadership, I show you how to get answers for serious existential crises that affect us all. Some of the questions I asked were about global leaders' duties. However, each of us are responsible for leading the way in our homes, families and communities. Hopefully this book introduces you to different perspectives on governing and leadership with ancient and now popular practices for making decisions that when used properly brings improved quality of life, peace, harmony abundance and true connection.

It is really each of us that have to make minute to minute decisions and choices every day that eventually affects everyone. This is because honestly we rarely think about government leaders, they are in offices only opened 9 AM to 5 PM, Monday through Friday located hundreds or thousands of miles away. Therefore, we have the responsibility for our own lives and to know what is going on in the world around us too.

The other way that this book, Decisions Decisions Volume 5: Governance and Leadership, is different is that my previous books were written years after the spiritual guidance messages. This book is written as the events are happening. This has meant me having to be attentive to the news and open to differences in perspectives, as well as my intuition. I invite you to come along on the journey.

It is what happened on January 6, 2021, that gave me the push to write this book, <u>Decisions Decisions: Getting Answers for Life's Challenges</u>. The prediction for the events of that day, and its unfolding sequel were initially to be in the beginning chapter of Volume 1, not instead in Volume 5 at the end of the book. However, we are still waiting for the outcome of many crises and challenges during this presidential term. Come along on the journey.

PART ONE: THE PRESIDENCY

Chapter 1: Deciding Who to Vote For President

On March 17, 2020 in preparation for the primary elections, I did an IChing reading asking for higher guidance and insight into who would be the best presidential leader for the United States of America:

Bernard (Bernie) Sanders?

Hexagram 48: The Well, lines 3 and 5 into hexagram 7: The Army. Hexagram 48 has the image of a village well. Water from a well provides nourishment for all who come and go regardless of where they live.

Such a leader will have the potential for doing good deeds and rendering beneficial service. He would need to have the qualities of a teacher and a salesperson because consciously and unconsciously he would have to be continuously selling himself to others. He has the ability to influence others and his influence is far reaching. Nurturing others materially and spiritually. He will need to go with the flow and be adaptable, flexible, but resolute in his plans. Encourages others to better their personal lives as well as the community.

However, although his potential is great and he is well qualified, people are not making use of him. "An able person is available. He is like a purified well whose water is drinkable. But no use is made of him. Circumstances at this point has it that this person is not being used for the benefit of society. But even with this fate, just wait. Persevere in what is correct because it is a situation in transition. Don't give up. Keep persevering with what is correct. Time will come when he will move on up and proper use is made of him." He has the talent to become the leader of a nation, even a world leader, with a great love for the people. A humanitarian and a visionary. (Chu & Sherrill, 1976, 1993).

Hexagram 7 commonly referred to as the Army is also called Collective Power. This means the dynamic power of joint effort. He would need to broaden his ideals to include the goals of people around him in order to achieve his own aims. The situation needs cooperation and teamwork to overcome difficulties and achieve goals. If he is open, receptive and devoted to the needs and sentiments of others they will aid and support him. Success depends on inspiring a virtuous vision, discipline, organization and using ethical principles. Only a leader with a strong and persevering attitude, holding steadfast to inner truth and guidance can maintain such collective power. As with an army, everyone must follow orders although they may not understand why. Therefore, a correct and strong leader whose age, wisdom and experience automatically commands respect.

It is sad that others do not make use of Bernie Sanders. Perhaps because he tends to work alone, instead of as a team, therefore Joseph Biden may be the leader more able to bring the country together at this time.

Joseph (Joe) R. Biden, Jr.

Hexagram 12 Stagnation lines 4 and 6 into hexagram 8 Union. He will be a strong and wise leader with inner integrity that will automatically influence others to work with him. He will receive help from his colleagues. Biden has the potential ability to bring the United States of America out of its stagnant standstill, ending adverse conditions, and promoting peace. Because he understands the natural laws of change he will firmly bring new ways to achieve the country's goals. Biden is a spiritual person allowing his faith to guide him. He has the ability to unite the country.

Joe Biden Won the Election. Joseph Biden was voted the United States' 46th president on November 6, 2020 with more votes than previous presidents. At then 78 years old, he is also the oldest US president, with a background history of serving as senator for thirty-six years until he became vice president during 2009-2017 with President Barack Obama. With a 279 to 214 lead in the Electoral College votes, while some mail-in and absentee ballots were still being counted, it was declared he won the election.

Please Note: The interpretations and insights came from reading several IChing books, listed in the back of this book, that I used to summarize the main points here and in later chapters.

Chapter 2: Contested Election and Insurrection

Predictive Solstice Guidance

As usual for each Winter Solstice, on December 21st, 2020, I asked for higher guidance and insights into what I am to focus on for the next six months for improving my own life and fulfilling my destiny purpose:

IChing Hexagram 21 (line 2) Gnawing Through to Breakthrough into Hexagram 38 Opposition

Hexagram 21 Breakthrough. Gives guidance for overcoming obstacles and adverse conditions. The advice is given to leaders because it is up to leaders to to initiate, disseminate and enforce proper laws firmly and vigorously. The use of legislative, executive and judicial legal matters to correct situations. This is a time everyone needs to correct themselves or to be corrected. Hexagram 21 gives guidance on how corrections should be made. Offenders must be disciplined and punished especially those whose deliberate misconduct is interfering with the unity of the community. Forceful reforms are needed.

Line 2: Hardened criminals must be punished. Broad reforms needed to be initiated. However this must be done for the right purpose and punishment should not be cruel nor unjust.

As you can imagine, I was confused wondering what I might have done that would warrant discipline or punishment. Neither was I, a leader.

Hexagram 38. Opposition occurs when there are stubborn differences of opinion, perspectives, and decisions on what direction to take. The opposition must be removed gradually. Again there is a leader available who can provide some guidance. It is possible for these problems to be solved when participants are willing to become receptive to guidance and reduce emotions that cloud the truth of the situation.

Two weeks later, on January 6, 2021, I turned on the television for the weather forecast at 11:00 AM central standard time. I forgot that there were no regular television programs because Congress was counting the electoral college votes. As expected, but concerning, was the opposition to Arizona's and Pennsylvania's votes alluding to alleged voter fraud. Therefore the House and the Senate had to go off to their separate chambers to deliberate. This was unprecedented. It also allowed an extended delay in the vote certification process.

Meanwhile I watched, as over one thousand President Trump rally participants and protesters converged on the United States Capital building grounds, violently pushed past the barricades and police, climbed the scaffolding, scaled the walls of the Capitol up to the balconies, then broke through windows and doors to get to where Congress was convening to officially verify the electoral votes. Secret Service personnel herded Vice President Pence, members of Congress, and staff away to safety. They huddled scared, while texting tweets and other messages to their families. They begged and demanded President Trump tell his rioting supporters to go home, and to call in more security forces.

Cameras showed a few injured people. I thought perhaps someone fell off of the scaffolding, as they carried someone on a stretcher away from the crowd. From 1:00 pm to 8 pm, seven hours seemed like forever before National Guard troops got crowds under control and secured the Capital area. They formed a line of troops in full riot gear and as the crowd walked peacefully away, a curfew was declared for the entire city of Washington DC.

Of course, we were relieved. But as an African American, I couldn't help but wonder how people who caused so much damage and violence and threats to lawmakers were allowed to leave freely without being arrested. If it were a crowd of 'black or brown' complexion protesters, police in full riot gear and army tanks would have been there well in advance lining the streets, with their assault rifles, tasers and swat teams at the ready.

More frightening than watching the insurrection unfold on television was the realization of the potential for a worse situation than the riots at the

Capital — threats to US democracy with a coup attempt to insert an autocracy. Memories surfaced of the mockery of all our democracy symbols and international embarrassment during the past four years of the Trump administration. Seems he groomed the public for this day.

Chapter 3: Anniversary of the Insurrection

January 6, 2022

Below are excerpts from the transcripts of President Biden's speech on the anniversary of the insurrection January 6, 2022 that show President Biden's commitment to reuniting the country. He also made it clear to the United States and the world that he is committed to upholding the laws:

"I believe in the power of the presidency and the purpose is to unite this nation, not divide it; to lift us up, not tear us apart; to be about us — us, not about 'me.' But whatever my other disagreements are with Republicans who support the rule of law and not the rule of a single man, I will always seek to work together with them to find shared solutions when possible. Because if we have a shared belief and democracy than anything is possible — anything. And so, at this moment, we must decide: What kind of nation are we going to be?"

He asked the public to join him in his efforts to restore unity and maintain the integrity of our democracy:

"Look, folks, now it's up to all of us —"we the people" to stand for the rule of law, to preserve the flame of democracy to keep the promise of America alive. Both at home and abroad, we're engaged anew in a struggle between democracy and autocracy, between the aspirations of the many and the greed of the few, between the people's right of self-determination and [the] self - — the self-seeking autocrat. We reject the view of if you succeed, I fail; if you get ahead I fall behind; if I hold you down, I somehow lift myself up.

And with rights come responsibilities. The responsibility to see each other as neighbors. Maybe we disagree with that neighbor, but they are not an adversary. The responsibility to accept defeat then get back in the arena and try again the next time to make your case. The responsibility to see that America is an idea – an idea that requires visual stewardship.

CHAPTER 3: ANNIVERSARY OF THE INSURRECTION

Deep in the heart of America burns a flame lit almost 250 years ago — of liberty, freedom, and equality. This is not a land of kings, or dictators or autocrats. We are a nation of laws; of order, not chaos; of peace, not violence. Here in America, the people rule through the ballot, and their will prevails. So let's remember; together we're one nation, under God, indivisible, that today, tomorrow and forever, at our best, we are the United States of America."

Chapter 4: Investigation Begins

The 2020 IChing guidance reading, Hexagram 38 Opposition, continues to come true. Opposition occurs when there are stubborn differences of opinion, perspectives, and decisions on what direction to take. The opposition must be removed gradually. Again, there is a leader available who can provide some guidance. It is possible for these problems to be solved when participants are willing to become receptive to guidance and reduce emotions that cloud the truth of the situation.

CHAPTER 4: INVESTIGATION BEGINS

A second impeachment was tried on charges of "incitement of insurrection" for President Trump's role in the riots. Original purpose of impeachment in the Constitution was to prevent the abuse of power and remove the offending official. The House of Representatives voted on January 13, 2021 to try to impeach Trump a week before his presidential term ended. However, there were not enough votes in the Senate therefore their acquittal freed him again.

Throughout 2021, attempts to begin investigation into what happened on January 6, what led up to the insurrection, and who to prosecute were repeatedly obstructed by the opposition. Within Congress and within the general public the United States is a country greatly divided by economic classism, ethnic racism, and political parties of the Democrats versus the Republicans, with the Republicans putting forth the most obstacles. A threat to our democracy and unity.

On July 27, 2021, the Insurrection Select Committee to Investigate the January 6 Attack on the United States Capital was formed. The Department of Justice (DOJ) along with the Federal Bureau of Investigation (FBI) began gradually arresting participants identified through social media posts, witnesses, and photos that matched enlarged and highlighted pictures on the FBI's Most Wanted webpage. Thus far, 855 of the 2000 people that were involved in the riots were charged with federal crimes including conspiracy for planning the riot, violent attacks on police, or solely being part of the mob.

In fall of 2021, The House voted to hold two key Trump administration staff in contempt of Congress for refusing to testify in the investigation. Some progress in January 2022, when the Supreme Court ruled that Trump had to hand over documents concerning his communications and participation in the attacks on the Capital. The Department of Justice began arresting suspects for more serious charges of seditious conspiracy. On February 18, 2022, federal Judge Mehta ruled that former President Trump could be held accountable for inciting the attack on the US Capitol building during his pre-insurrection rally speech by going forward with three civil lawsuits filed by the attorney general of the District of Columbia for assaults on Democratic House members and Capital Police officers. Other court cases will proceed with linking allegations of conspiracy between Trump extremists and militia groups for planning and promoting violence.

Judge David Carter, on March 28, 2022 ordered the release of an additional one hundred communication documents to the Insurrection Select Committee after he ruled that former President Trump and his legal advisor John Eastman more likely than not, committed multiple federal crimes in their planned efforts to prevent Congress from certifying President Biden's 2020 election victory. President Trump and John Eastman could be charged with two felonies: obstruction of an official proceeding by spurring on the Capital riot, and conspiracy to defraud the United States by spreading election misinformation, further interfering in the election certification process while trying to persuade Vice President Pence to reject select states' electoral votes and delay proceedings by sending the counts back to the states. Judge Carter's ruling could put pressure on the Department of Justice to bring criminal charges against Trump and other high-level officials that were involved in trying to overturn the election.

On June 9, 2022, the Insurrection Select Committee to Investigate the January 6th Attack on the United States Capital, aired the first of eight public hearings during the summer, shown on evening primetime television channels. They presented new testimonies and evidence through witnesses and videos to build the case to indict President Trump for his involvement in planning, instigating and exciting the insurrection, then not doing anything to stop it as he saw the violence unleashed for hours. The public watched as videos showed alleged extremist white supremacy military groups arrive early to the Capitol building before President Trump's rally was over, and as later the several thousands of rioters in one mass strategically attacked the Capitol building from all sides. It would be difficult to not see this as an attempted coup, usually seen in other countries.

More shocking is that for three hours, the then President Trump did nothing to stop the mob attacks and rioting at the Capitol building. Instead he was in the White House dining room watching the riot on television. He ignored his national security advisers and senior staff, even his family and long-time friends, and also the press who continuously begged him to tell the rioters to stop. But he refused, although he was the only one who could really call the siege off.

President Trump also refused to call in backups for the Secret Service and the Capitol police. Vice President Pence had to take on the duties of directing and ordering in the military National Guard troops. Meanwhile the lives of the Vice President and legislators were threatened as the rioters were breaking into the inner chambers and there was teargas in the hallway. President Trump's advisers urged him to make a public peaceful transfer of power. They had to eventually threaten him with the 25th amendment of future impeachment for dereliction of his duties, and violation of his presidential oath. Then Trump reluctantly agreed to make an announcement but not the recommended pre-written speech to announce his acceptance of the election results. Instead, he still talked about voter fraud, a landslide election in his favor, for which there was no evidence.

I, along with the most of rest of the United States citizens watched in repulsed horror as the Select

CHAPTER 4: INVESTIGATION BEGINS

Committee showed videos and heard testimonies of the brutality and unbelievable viciousness with which the rioters with improvised and military weapons attacked and humiliated the Capital and D.C. police. Several policemen died during, and immediately after the January 6th insurrection. Some later from suicide.

Department of Justice judges are using evidence from the Congressional hearings to prosecute those involved, including President Trump, in the attacks at the Capitol building. In October 2022, the Insurrection Select Committee voted unanimously to subpoena Trump to testify under oath and bring relevant documents. This was intended to provide further assurance that no future president could succeed at anything even remotely similar to the unlawful steps Trump took to overturn the election.

Of course, Trump failed to appear for his disposition hearing on November 14, 2022. Instead he filed a lawsuit asking courts to protect him from giving testimony, although his attempts to do this in previous courts were rejected repeatedly. He argued that there should be separation of power between the legislative, judicial and the executive branches. It is true that when the Constitution was drafted, it instructed that there be a separation of between the three branches of government, with the initial intent to provide ways of checks and balances to prevent one sector of the government from overpowering another branch.

CHAPTER 4: INVESTIGATION BEGINS

This was to ensure the liberties of the United States' people. Ironically, the main purpose was to also prevent too much authority by a single leader or group. Throughout his presidential term Trump managed to make a mockery of our whole democratic system by overstepping the boundaries of laws, and threatening the liberties of the people, especially on January 6, 2020 to get whatever he wanted. So how would we now prove that no president is above the law?

As usual Trump was stalling for time since he knew that the insurrection Select Committee will probably be dissolved in January 2023, as the House becomes a Republican majority. It is possible that the Senate will form another investigative committee.

After gathering enough evidence from witnesses' and participants' testimonies, the Justice Department went after the ringleaders from extremist groups. On November 29, 2022 the jury and judge declared Oath Keeper founder Steward Rhodes and his deputy Kelly Megg guilty of seditious conspiracy with a prison sentence of up to 20 years in prison. Rhodes was later sentenced to 18 years, although he didn't enter the Capitol building on January 6, he allegedly was outside sending communications between his recruited members. There was evidence that he had helped with strategically planning the insurrection since the November election results, months in advance, for the use of force and weapons. Other members of the

Oath Keepers and Proud Boys groups were also charged and awaited trials.

The Select Committee released the following statement: "It's vital that there be accountability for every vile act of January 6 and the events that led to that day's tragedy. We applaud the Justice Department's success today and support ongoing efforts to ensure accountability at all levels."

In July 2022 the Senate drafted the bill S4573 Electoral Count Reform and Presidential Improvement Transition Act of 2022 to emphasize that the vice president has no power to change the electoral vote count as his role is only a ministerial procedure, and there needs to be at least one-fifth of congressional members to object. Later in September 2022 the House of

Representatives proposed and passed HR8873 Presidential Election Reform Act indicates no State can delay election day nor the certification of votes by state governors, and there needs to be at least one-third of congressional members to object. Both bipartisan bills are intended to close the loopholes in the old Electoral Count Act of 1887 that allow it to be misinterpreted and exploited. No longer would solely one person from each House's objections be considered enough. On December 29, 2022 President Biden signed the Electoral Count Reform Act into law as part of the $1.7 trillion federal spending package for 2023.

During the last week of 2022, the Select Committee provided public transcripts of witness testimonies that were collected during the investigations. These records are available on the Select Committee's website with a link to the Final Report. They made several recommendations:

Criminal referrals to the Department of Justice regarding charging former President Trump with obstruction of an official proceeding, conspiracy to defraud the United States, conspiracy to make false statements, and of his and other's involvement in inciting and assisting in an insurrection against the authority of the United States as he violated several statuses of United States Code Title 18 of the United States Constitution. This would bar former President Trump and others that were involved in the January 6 insurrection from ever holding federal office again. Further stronger criminal penalties for all those involved, federal penalties for those who threaten election workers, legislation to enforce congressional House subpoenas in federal court, and more oversight over the Capitol Police force as provisions in the spending package for more recruits, better training, equipment and communication to prevent future attempts of obstructions to the electoral process, domestic violence or rebellions.

Unfortunately not so fast, as Trump has used his money and political advantage to get lawyers to appeal by finding more loopholes in laws and ways to delay court dates. He also jeopardized national security as his speeches continued to incite others to make threats against court staff and their families.

Donald Trump was indicted on August 1st, 2023 by federal grand jury for attempting to overturn the results of the 2020 election. He was charged with four felony counts:

1. Conspiracy to defraud the United States by spreading false claims about the November election being stolen.

2. Conspiracy to obstruct an official proceeding by alleged planning starting immediately after the November 2020 election up through January 2021 to disrupt the electoral vote certification on January 6, 2021.

3. Obstruction of and attempt to obstruct an official proceeding along

with his co-conspirators on January 6, 2021.

4. Conspiracy against citizens rights as Trump and his co-conspirators allegedly attempted to "oppressed, threaten and intimidate" people to try to prevent them from voting and in the election.

In addition, other indictments were brought against Donald Trump:

Classified document case. He is accused of bringing top-secret documents at his estate.

Hush money scheme case. For allegedly falsifying financial business documents.

Harassment. Although he appealed, a judge ordered him to pay an additional $83 million for continued social media verbal attacks against an alleged former sexual assault victim.

Georgia election fraud case. He's accused of trying to persuade Georgia lawmakers to find extra votes, of harassing election workers and trying to appoint and replace electoral college electors.

Starting in December 2023, individual States again attempted to block Trump from being on the primary ballots as a presidential candidate. According to Section 3 of the 14th Amendment, former federal, state, and military officials who have engaged in "insurrection or rebellion" against the United States are to be barred from ever holding office again (Fredrickson, Neff, 2021). Yet as of February 2024, Trump is still the Republican presidential candidate front runner in spite of these attempts to prosecute him.

Therefore, the IChing Hexagram 21 advice and universe's will is being done, although United States' government leaders may or may not have known or done their own spiritual readings for guidance. Congress took the lead to initiate, use legislative knowledge to gather and disseminate evidence to pressure executive and judicial branches of the government to take action legally to pass reforms and enforce proper laws firmly and vigorously. This investigation process took eighteen months of consistent effort. Offenders continue to be disciplined and punished especially those whose deliberate misconduct is interfering with the unity of the nation. Trump still has more court trials to go to.

PART TWO: OTHER CHALLENGES OF THE BIDEN PRESIDENCY

Chapter 5: COVID-19 and the Economy

3-17-20. Please give higher guidance and insight into the situation regarding the coronavirus COVID-19 pandemic and economy of the United States:

IChing: Hexagram 46 Ascending Coming Up. This is a step-by-step process that has supreme success when we strive for and follow what's right and correct while letting go of anxieties and fears. Seeking spiritual guidance eliminates fears. The image is of a recently planted young tree. Knowing that trees grow slowly, so we too have to be patient and persistent so that the results will be positive and long-lasting. A time of progressive, gradual upward movement. This hexagram also represents the people, meaning working together with the public, keeping the people's needs in focus. By continuously getting clarity on what has to be done, the way is open for us to succeed with these challenges.

There aren't any specific guidance lines stressed, since we have only have one hexagram, we can look at line 5, which is the role of the leader: Able leaders who administer their duties and responsibilities efficiently step-by-step. These are natural leaders who have developed their leadership through learning and wisdom gained from experience. After decades of experience, President Biden definitely has expertise from assisting and observing several presidential administrations.

Line 2 also mentions qualifications of the leadership required to resolve the pressing issues of the COVID pandemic and the economy. Authentic sincerity of the President is to be shown in everything he does. He will need the loyalty of other leaders, as well as Congress and his White House administration. And it actually does say that using the faith gained from ancient wisdom will for sure further progress.

Sacred Path Cards: 8 East Shield Illumination/Clarity is the need for and ability to open to the truth, with new understanding and personal inner knowing. Seeking what's right for improving the conditions in the United States. Instead of being stuck in old ways so long that we stop believing there are other options. What do we value the most? Eagle is the symbol of the East Shield. Can we raise up high enough above, to see the overall picture of our situation? A balanced, equal society means valuing everyone's ideas, talents, and creativity along with knowing that everything we do is an exchange of energy that goes beyond our illusion of the power of dollar bills. True freedom.

So what decisions need to be made?

On 4-21-21. A friend asked this question: Will the United States government be able to move in the appropriate direction to restore balance and institute equality? So we sought guidance with the IChing :

Hexagram 49 Revolution/Change (lines one and six) into hexagram 33 Retreat.

Hexagram 49. Change is inevitable. People tend to resist change, so leaders have to be able to know when the time is right, persevere, and increase public faith and belief in the necessity for change, by leaders being correct in their own actions and knowledge.

Line1: It best to wait to make major changes until the time is right. Meanwhile prepare a firm foundation to move forward later.

Line 6: Those who have less experience for governance should step back to allow leaders with the appropriate strategies for the situation to follow through on implementing what has already been decided and proven to be effective, without interfering. Although radical changes are needed there is strong resistance from those who don't yet understand.

Hexagram 33 means to retreat temporarily and return later.

Initially, I was confused about what "revolution" referred to, besides the riots on January 6, 2021. Perhaps it has been more of a quiet gradual internal personal transformation of individuals' revolution taken place rather than external protests. Then it occurred to me later in 2021, that perhaps a revolution started with the COVID shutdown, before the election as people had time to reflect on their priorities in life. Not knowing who would live, or what businesses would survive, people were no longer willing to sacrifice time away from precious family to be disrespected and taken advantage of by employers and corporations. Hence the Great Resignation, also known as the Great Quit or the Great Reshuffle is an example of people taking personal action without a leader persuading them. They simply emotionally and physically had had enough, and couldn't or wouldn't push themselves anymore.

But I was wrong. It was to be more than internal personal changes, as the

United States was made aware of how close we came to a real revolution on January 6th.

Chapter 6: Unalienable Rights

After two more mass shootings occurred within a week's time in May 2022, people are asking and having discussions about "What can be done to prevent more mass shootings?" Several mass shootings again the following weekend in June. How can an 18-year-old or anyone be allowed to purchase an AR-15 semiautomatic assault rifle and excessive ammunition fifteen rifle magazine cartridges of 30 rounds each, yet the store clerk not have warning feelings about it? And be able to sleep at night? How can 18-year-old adolescents, who can't legally buy alcohol and cigarettes until they are 21 years old, be considered responsible enough to own an assault weapon? Does raising the age to 21 solve the problem, when it was adolescents in their 20's who did the earlier mass shootings at Virginia Tech, Sandy Hook in Connecticut, First Baptist Church in Texas, and a Walmart in Texas?

Mass shootings bring temporary national attention to gun violence. However, 111 people are killed each day in the United States by gun violence. This adds up to over 40,000 people dying each year. With guns readily available more people died by suicide, by murders intentional or unintentional, and as intimate partner domestic violence deaths increased threefold during the COVID pandemic shutdowns. To answer the question on most people's minds, "What can be done to decrease gun violence in the United States," it occurred to me to rather than lose more sleep worrying, why not do spiritual oracle readings to seek higher guidance.

5/29/22. Please give higher guidance and insight into what the United States should do to decrease mass shootings and other gun violence:

Metu Neter Cards: Maat tu tchaas / Sebek tu tchaas.

Tu tchaas indicates that leaders and people do know something about what needs to be done. We know at least intellectually (Sebek) how to share, we showed we can occasionally be generous like we did at the beginning of the COVID pandemic. Starting to realize that what we each do, affects all living beings in the world as resources and the climate declines due to us disobeying Maat natural laws therefore suffering (Herukhuti) consequences. However, we've lost faith (Maat) that we can change the situation by changing what is in our hearts. Bringing peace, calm, and most importantly true love to those who feel abandoned by families and society. Who, otherwise could lonesomely strike out violently in despair and hopelessness? We've given up our power to leaders who refused to seek and follow divine guidance because it would mean having the Herukhuti concept of courage to sacrifice for what is right for all the people. Forgotten that abundance and all we need, does not come from other people, it comes from the Universe. We each have more than enough, certainly more than people in other countries, including more freedoms. However without connection, purpose, self-discipline and guidance we tend to self-destruct.

IChing: Hexagram 53 lines 1 and 5 into hexagram 63.

Hexagram 53 Gradual Development. This is a time of gradual, not rapid growth but of course we want change NOW. Although the thought of trying to do anything about gun violence seems daunting and overwhelming hexagram 53 indicates that change is possible. This can be done by reprogramming and influencing our unseen unconscious towards positive societal values. We've already been subliminally and blatantly programmed from the television, movies, video games, music lyrics, YouTube, Facebook, etc, by companies who make huge profits by trying to get us to accept violence and disrespect as normal. We could instead make the choice to reverse this trend by portraying positive images of genuine cooperation, communication, purpose and sharing. In the United States, we have freedom to do most anything that we want, so why not make the choice to focus on putting efforts on positive goals not senseless rebelling. Okay, okay, for how many years of our lives do we have to keep proving, that because the laws say you are not an adult until you are eighteen or twenty-one years old that you shouldn't drink, smoke, have sex, or steal – that we can get away with murder? Is this normal responsible adult behavior?

To fix the gun violence problem, long-term goals with proven strategies and ongoing implementation of plans are essential. Intellectual, communicative abilities combined with the innate wisdom of leaders with extraordinary honest attributes are required, who will sacrifice for the benefit of all.

Line 1: Yes, this will be challenged with resistance, habits can be stubborn, with initial increased danger from the opposition but we will have to ignore the criticism, fears, and doubts by proceeding steadily forward anyway if the United States and the rest of the world is to survive.

Lines 6: The United States' success in bringing peace, equality, and therefore decreasing reasons for gun violence will inspire other countries to follow our example. European countries, such as the United Kingdom after its first and only school shooting, immediately passed stricter gun control laws and took away guns in private homes. However, only taking away guns is not enough. The United Kingdom and other European countries have more social nets such as low cost to free healthcare, college tuition, daycare, eldercare and parental leave, so there is less debt and less stress. We've been opposed to higher taxes based on income. Yet, there has to be other options. Europe has similar concerns about the mental health and suicides of their youth with contributing factors of video gaming, lack of sleep, emphasis on high grades in schools and bullying.

Hexagram 63 After Completion. Seriously folks, this means that we can be successful in decreasing gun violence, because the title of this hexagram is "after completion." It gives guidance on what to do after you achieve your goals. Movement out of disorder into order is complete. However, there will be a natural tendency for us to only partially understand, since we are learning a new way of living and being. Therefore, there is danger of making mistakes.

Gradually, balance will be achieved, as the old ways ends and a new natural cycle begins, put in motion as the universe also helps in our favor. However, we will have to continue and maintain the strategies that have made this condition of now being in balance towards a peaceful world successful. Cautiously, paying more attention to details, correcting mistakes and anticipating foreseeable challenges prevents backsliding.

People with high status and leadership need to continue to help the public. Knowing that there are people who will try to resist and challenge the new changes, we cannot get too relaxed and allow disorder to creep back in. Ongoing planning and firm enforcement of correct behavior is required.

Sacred Path Cards: 11 North Shield Wisdom and Gratitude.

This card encourages us to continue to transcend and to live truth. Wisdom and solutions to challenges comes from listening to different cultural ideas and ways of doing, sharing as we seek to understand the much larger world around us. Learning from life experiences as well as respect for and cherishing our elders' wisdom. Again, we are being reminded to pay attention to the natural laws of the universe, and the intuitive guidance we receive from ancestors who have gone on before us. Quietly observing truth and the rhythmic patterns for yourself and not doubting what you see.

Each person is responsible for own behavior, regardless of what legislative laws are made. We are the ones who live in our bodies and can make the choice of having inner peace and clarity of thinking. Washington DC and State capitals are hundreds and thousands of miles away. Legislators don't live in our homes and communities. For example and analogy, if there is a lot of litter on the ground, who put it there? And who leaves it there? We cannot blame others for what we are not doing ourselves. It's time to seek healing and forgiveness – of ourselves and others. And for all of us to walk our talk! We do each have unalienable rights and free will, but with that comes personal responsibility.

Tarot Cards:

I pulled three cards for the overview of the mass shooting situation, our challenge, and what action is needed.

Overview of situation: VIII of Swords. From the interpretation in the book, Holistic Tarot, my understanding is that this is a situation of people feeling unjustly trapped and stuck with no way out. But when we really are truthful with ourselves, we realize that there are no real physical restraints. Our eyes are just closed refusing to look at alternative solutions. Together we could support each other, but each of us feels like a lonely victim of our perceived circumstances. This sword card is upside down, reversed, indicating that relief is coming, as we change our thinking. There will be emancipation. And we realize that it could've been much worse.

Challenge: XVII The Star. The challenge asked of us of is more of an inner individual choice to change how we personally want to perceive the world and our emotions. The Star represents hope, inspiration, good mental health, abundance, and harmony. These along with inner peace is what spiritual abundance is about. Generously sharing of what you have, true love and compassion along with sharing your natural talents. You'll recognize this again as the basic principles of Maat. Knowing a bright and hopeful future awaits us. By renewing our hope and optimism then true self-empowerment occurs by following higher guidance that comes from within each of us. Deep breathing and meditating helps bring our desired conscious goals of living in a safe peaceful world, to our unconscious to be able to automatically take action with appropriate behavior and self-control.

Each of us, during the past few years since 2019 have suffered and toiled personally and collectively with the chaos of several crises happening all at once. Many have lost hope. The good news is we are now ready and prepared to move into a brighter future. The Star card is also reversed and explains that the United States has become too pessimistic and cynical which is affecting all of our mental and physical health. It's not normal to live in fear, especially when we as a country have much to be grateful for. Intellectually, we get depressed by constant media's pessimistic ideologies. We need to reverse these negative messages. Enough is enough! From a young age we've been taught to feel empty, bored, and as worthless victims in a competitive, fast-paced, technological, heavily indebted society that makes it hard for anyone to keep up.

Even more so than the indebtedness is the feeling that our leaders and corporations don't really care about us. During the COVID pandemic, while some workers got to work from home, "essential workers" had to stay on the job without enough masks, gloves, and other personal protective equipment (PPE).

Medical providers already stretched thin before the COVID pandemic were pushed to the breaking point. Risking their own health as they were expected to work long shifts overtime, often six days straight with little sleep as they watched others die, making themselves more susceptible to acquiring COVID, high blood pressure, diabetes, etc. Suicide rates among doctors increased. Years of schooling and experience down the drain as other nurses and doctors retired early, left the health field, or are still suffering with a long haul COVID symptoms or worse may become permanently disabled. Who will fill the gap in hospitals and clinics while waiting for new graduates to replace them? Observing current working conditions who would even want to? Insurances and for-profit hospitals paying less and making health care providers blink once at 30 to 40 patients a day, causing discouraged patients to stay away. If this is how those with traditional prestigious status are treated, it's not hard to imagine what other essential worker's wages and working conditions are. Longer and longer commutes, while working several jobs. Continuous unnecessary stress and frustration.

This results in parents not having time or energy to be with their families, and when they do, frustration may be released onto their children, spouses and other significant others. Included in mass shootings statistics are the men who lose their jobs and then come home and kill their whole family and then themselves. Mothers who attempt similar go to prison. We need government and public supports beyond money towards emotionally and physically safe families, communities, schools, and workplaces.

We've held onto deep pains from past generations' trauma's for far too long. Is it really any wonder that people have felt trapped physically and emotionally in situations that they feel they can't get out of? It really isn't a problem of one group of people distrusting another group of people as much as no one feels safe, accepted and truly valued just as they are. If we don't constantly achieve and make plenty money, then we are always on the verge of losing our fortunes with businesses collapsing and being thrown out onto the streets as a nobody. How much stress can people take before giving up and taking it out on somebody else, even innocent children? Any release valve would have difficulty holding back all that frustration and despair. No, this behavior isn't from mental illness! Unless you want to acknowledge that our whole country and its leadership is not well.

Action: V The Hierophant advices us on what we need to do to resolve the challenges of our situation. The Hierophant card represents tradition, institutions, conventionalism and conformity. In the United States we label politicians as "conservative" or liberal. But is this true? Most of us are pressured into conformity and to hide one's differences. There's been a lot of deceptions and lies told to the public by political parties, organizations, and corporations. Status and societal approval becomes more important to them, instead of doing what is right. True leaders would have wisdom, learn from life experience, seek and follow divine knowledge. While having the good intention of maintaining, but by misinterpreting the second amendment, we are harming others by only protecting a few people's "rights." The Hierophant card in reverse encourages nonconformity, self-determination, and being unconventional.

Eleven days after I sought spiritual guidance, on June 9, 2022, Chairman Thompson of the Insurrection Select

Committee to Investigate the January 6th Attack on the United States Capital used similar words to appeal to the American public and the world:

"January 6th and the lies that led to insurrection have put two and a half centuries of constitutional democracy at risk. The world is watching what we do here. America has long been expected to be a shining city on a hill. A beacon of hope and freedom. A model for others, when we are at our best. How can we play that role when our house is in such disorder?"

The House Judicial Committee voted on June 8th to pass gun control bill H.R.7910 "Protecting Our Kids Act." Amendments were made to previous legislation to increase the age limit to 21, to prevent purchases of certain semiautomatic centerfire rifles, modifications to make other guns semiautomatic, large capacity ammunition devices, buying guns for others, prohibition on untraceable firearms and gun trafficking, and to encourage safe storage of firearms. It was thought doubtful, yet hopeful that the Senate also passes the bill.

The following weekend, thousands of people gathered for March for Our Lives protests on the National Mall in Washington DC, and in other cities and towns across the United States on Saturday, June 11, 2022, to demand gun violence reform. We the People's power to affect change. Obviously, legal age had nothing to do with access to guns and other weapons for violence during the January 6 attack on the United States Capitol. Role-modeling for young people how to resolve disagreements, conflicts, and to get what you want? Even if it means everyone losing everything? A very chilling reality check for all of us.

Now is the time to restore hope in humanity's ability to solve our collective problems.

During November 2022, again three more mass shootings within two weeks. These were the mass shootings that were national news. Definition of a mass shooting is four or more people killed or injured, not including the shooter. In actuality there were 87 mass shootings in October and 43 in November. More than 648 total mass shootings for the year, averaging 100 deaths a day, according to the Gun Violence Archive.org.

Doctors marched again to the United States Capitol to reinforce that "gun violence is a public health crisis" an emergency, as gun violence is now the leading cause of death for children and teens.

(Please note that the above are brief summaries of events from as close to original sources as possible. For details, you can do further research with links to websites and articles referenced in the back of this book).

Chapter 7: President Biden's Second State of the Union Address

True to the IChing description of the personal characteristics and purpose of Biden being chosen for presidency, he included in his speech the following excerpts:

" You know, we're often told that Democrats and Republicans can't work together. But over the past two years we proved the cynics and the naysayers wrong. Yes, we disagreed plenty. And yes, there were times when Democrats had to go it alone.

CHAPTER 7: PRESIDENT BIDEN'S SECOND STATE OF...

But time and again, Democrats and Republicans came together. (He gave some examples). In fact, I signed over 300 bipartisan laws since becoming president. To my Republican friends, if we could work together in the last Congress, there is no reason we can't work together in this new Congress. The people sent us a clear message, fighting for the sake of fighting, power for the sake of power, conflicts for the sake of conflicts, gets us nowhere.

And that's always been my vision for the country to restore the soul of the nation, to rebuild the backbone of America – the middle class. To unite the country."

Do you remember the prediction from the IChing when I sought guidance on who to vote for, Bernie Sanders or Joe Biden?

'IChing hexagram 12 Stagnation lines 4 and 6 into hexagram 8 Union.

He will be a strong and wise leader with inner integrity that will automatically influence others to work with him. He will receive help from his colleagues. Biden has the potential ability to bring the United States of America out of its stagnant standstill, ending adverse conditions, and promoting peace. Because he understands the natural laws of change, he will firmly bring new ways to achieve the country's goals. Biden is a spiritual person allowing his faith to guide him. He has the ability to unite the country.'

President Biden, of course, hasn't been able to fully unite the country in two short years, while surrounded by opposition and crises but he sure is courageously trying. We can all see with our own eyes he inherited economic and global woes from previous decades. Yet, for political reasons others blame him for not correcting these problems immediately. President Biden went on to tell us in his second State of the Union Address how he would accomplish these goals:

"We also need more first responders and professionals to address the growing mental health, substance abuse challenges. More resources to reduce violent crime and gun crime. More community intervention programs. More investments in housing, education and job training. All this can prevent violence in the first place."

"And we pay for these investments in our future by finally making the wealthiest and the biggest corporations begin to pay their fair share. I am a capitalist. But just pay your fair share. And I think a lot of you at home agree with me that our present tax system is simply unfair. The idea that in 2020, fifty-five of the biggest companies in America made $40 billion in profits and paid zero in federal income taxes? That's simply not fair. But now, because of the law I signed, billion-dollar companies have to pay a minimum of 15%. Just 15%. That's less than a nurse pays. Let me be clear. Under my plan, nobody earning less than $400,000 a year will pay an additional penny in taxes. Nobody. Not one penny. But there is more to do. Let's finish the job. Reward work, not just wealth. Pass my proposal for a billionaire millionaire minimum tax. Because no billionaires should pay a lower tax rate than a teacher or a firefighter."

President Biden is inching us closer to a peaceful, equal society.

Chapter 8: World Peace

True Democracy

Paramount in indigenous cultures, ongoing developing of good character is expected. Guidance begins in early childhood learning that whatever anyone does affects the whole community. Good character, humility, and respect for both the earth and community naturally controls excessive behaviors. Leaders must have good character as the main criteria for selection.

According to the elders in the book, <u>Guardians of the Soil: Meeting</u>

<u>Zimbabwe's Elders</u>, kings of old insured that the people's needs and happiness were fulfilled. Therefore, when the people were happy the king was happy. Leaders listened in humbleness to everyone. It was a disgrace for anyone to be hungry. Food was equally distributed. Neighbors cared for each other.

Zimbabwean leaders in olden days, if they had more wealth, did not flaunt their wealth as status above other people. On the contrary, they dressed and lived same as their community. They listened to the voices and wisdom of their elders through spirit mediums and divination to make decisions above their own opinions.

The United States tells the world that democracy is when the public is able to vote. But what good is voting if the candidates to choose from, are not the best possible person for presidency or other government official positions? The best person for leadership does what is needed for the whole and puts the needs of the community first. Not who has the most money and knows other people with money and their families. The best person to lead the country may be found in a inner city neighborhood, on a Native American reservation or community, a small rural farm, an urban middle-class neighborhood or an immigrant or migrant worker. Perhaps the best person with the needed good personal character and leadership qualities is poor or of modest means. They may not be well academically educated.

War in Afghanistan

As the controversy continues as to whether President Biden should have pulled the troops out of Afghanistan or not, think about it for yourself. A region that has had endless wars. Their people hungry, starving, homeless, constantly afraid and stressed. President Biden stated in his July 8, 2021 speech, "And it's the right and responsibility of the Afghan people alone to decide their future and how they want to run their country. . . We're going to engage in a determined diplomacy to pursue peace and a peace agreement that will end this senseless violence."

He further emphasized this on August 16, 2021 "Our mission in Afghanistan was never supposed to be nation building. It was never supposed to be creating a unified, centralized democracy... We gave them every chance to determine their own future. What we could not provide for them was the will to fight for that future... If the political leaders of Afghanistan were unable to come together for the good of their people. Unable to negotiate for the future of their country when the chips were down, they would never have done it while U.S. troops remained in Afghanistan bearing the brunt of the fighting for them. We will continue to support the Afghan people. We will lead with our diplomacy, our international influence and our humanitarian aid. We'll continue to push for a regional diplomacy and engagement to prevent violence and instability... I have been clear that human rights must be the center of our foreign policy, not the periphery. But the way to do it is not through endless military deployment; it's with our diplomacy, our economic tools and rallying the world to join us."

Extending the President's message further, it is time for the civil wars within each country to stop. For people to stop fighting each other. And that includes the violence and discrimination within the United States. The insurrection attempt on January 6, 2021 showed the world that the United States is also a country divided. Although the world was shown the results of centuries of blatant systemic racism in 2020, the insurrection was white people fighting each other. Debates and media coverage over how the COVID-19 pandemic and natural disasters were managed also exposed the United States' own vulnerabilities to environmental challenges. There was neglect, misdirected blame, and inaction during the four and a half years of the previous presidential administration. No, these basic needs and societal problems are not new, but was allowed to worsen due to wasted hours of bickering among government officials for the past 12 years. Was Trump put in office for entertainment and distraction to hide the serious trouble the United States and the rest of the world is in? Is the infighting due to a sense of helplessness? Of feeling overwhelmed not knowing what to do? Or not knowing what decisions to make?

Famine

Often, it is when there are food shortages that civil wars and wars between countries occur. Fighting over other resources such as water, the fear of scarcity makes people desperate. When my great-uncle said, "Wars are about population control," I was upset with him and replied, 'That's an awful cruel way of thinking.' He served in WWWII, in Tuskegee Alabama repairing airplanes. The Army was about to deploy him just before the war was declared over. Now that I'm older, I understand why attempts at population control may make sense.

We, who are old enough, remember when Florida and California and southern states provided year round farming. Tell me where is our food coming from now that we over-farmed and ruined the soil causing drought, then forest fires, the western areas that were our breadbasket has floods, blizzards and freezing weather goes down south that were forecasted for the northern midwest United States? We built shopping malls, mansions and suburban subdivisions where there used to be woods and farms, killed off bees with pesticides, ruined other countries' soil and water too.

I will always remember the Zimbabwean elder who angrily asked me, "How can you dislike any food?" This was after I unthinkingly did not buy guavas from him and told him that it was because, "I don't like guavas." He went on to say, "We eat the corn while it's in season this time of year. After that's gone, we eat what's next." Their corn was very long with big kernels but tough. Suffering through another year of drought in Zimbabwe, his words of wisdom and anger made sense.

In the United States, we're spoiled. Our grocery shelves, meat, fish and deli cases, and produce sections with fruits and vegetables are always full and beautifully displayed. Boxes and bags of dried and frozen food are stored in our home kitchens. Those of us who are not farmers, we don't respect the harvest. We overeat and throw food away, not knowing or caring what happens when there is too little or too much rain or sunshine. Or too many insects like locusts eating up the crops and trees.

Even while we watch worsening raging forest fires, dry cracked hard dirt, or hurricanes, floods, and blizzards across the United States our store shelves are full. So where are we getting our "abundant" food from? Read the labels on packages and fresh produce. You'll see that most of the food now comes from other countries.

We have many immigrants coming from Mexico and Central America because the United States ruined their soil too, with erosion from over planting. From our greed—evident in our obesity–that only rich kings and queens used to have. We call the migrants and immigrants bad names, blaming them, making their lives miserable, while arrogantly barely paying them for their labor.

Unappreciative of their sacrifices so that we may have food on our tables while they go hungry and homeless. During the COVID crisis we called them "essential workers" yet don't seem to care as overworked, hungry and stressed they succumbed worldwide to the pandemic. Who will be left to grow and harvest food? What naturally nutrient soil will remain? Who will survive?

If we had kept our indigenous cultural spirituality and divination systems, we would have known to predict and prepare for famine ahead of time. But would we have listened? Meteorologists scientists also warned for decades of the effects of climate changes especially along the coasts. Yet no serious effort to evacuate populations at risk to higher ground. Biden signed the historic bipartisan infrastructure law, on April 28, 2023 to help protect people from natural disasters by repairing and building roads, bridges, levees, flood walls, power grids, stronger resilient homes and buildings along with repairing evacuation routes. Is it too late to mend our ways and plan now for the next seven generations?

Economic collapse is inevitable, because a monetary innovative corporate system is not sustainable, not only because of the effect on the environment but also on people. Go faster and faster, except humans are not robots. Eventually exhaustion and burnout occurs. Plus how much more stuff can we fit in our homes? Stuff that is purposely designed to break in two weeks, maybe a year or two if we are lucky, instead of when previously appliances lasted 15 to 20 years or more.

I had a Sear's clothing iron that lasted 12 years. Now days when the warranty is up in one year, it breaks the very next day. The young people don't know what this was like, as many adults are still living with their parents! My great uncle, who passed away at 96 years old, used his rotary telephone until it finally broke maybe five years before he died. Imagine how much money he saved over the years? Cars lasted decades too, now our computers' and cell phones' bills are what used to be car notes, except we can never pay them off!

At least back in the day, people had gardens and knew how to make their own clothes, fix their own cars and whatever else machinery because it had nuts and bolts. I knit socks, mittens, hats, sweaters, and I taught myself to make a quilt last year because I got tired of cheap thin fake "fabrics" and being cold. But what are our young people to do to survive? Money does no good if land, farmers and harvesters are gone. There will just be empty shelves same as in other countries.

Old timer leaders stuck in the past with old strategies like war aren't useful today. Autocratic dictator leaders become a figment of their own imagination as wars destroy infrastructure, homes, businesses, schools, farms, ruins the economy as civilians flee, and few people will come into a warring country to buy goods or trade. Fighting over results of elections while the people suffer. How can they beat their chest, shouting that they are the rightful leader, when "their" country essentially doesn't exist anymore?

Instead of fighting, we should be focusing on how to save the earth resources that still exist. And to share these resources with each other. Otherwise those who don't have, will find ways in desperation to steal from others who are greedily holding on to access. Then as we are seeing, – everyone is losing. As we all stand idly by and watch it all collapse around us. Obviously what we have been doing is not working. time for us to change.

When there's truly equality around the globe, then the viruses, addictions and other life-threatening illnesses that are an expression of our inner conflict between what we know to be true and what we are experiencing, these ills will simply disappear. There has to be an inner will to live, to live a full life. Otherwise life is not worth living. All the medicines and the vaccines and herbs and buying more stuff are no substitute for a better world to live in.

PART THREE: ANOTHER WORLD WAR?

Chapter 9: Russia Invasion of Ukraine

Russian President Vladimir Putin had been talking about invading Ukraine for about six months but I still was surprised when he actually followed through on February 24, 2022 with a premeditated, unprovoked, and unjustifiable full-scale war against Ukraine. In response, the United States immediately deployed military personnel to other countries close by in Europe to provide support and training but not to join the war.

Secretary of State Antony Blinken made a press release speech. Here is an excerpt:

"We salute the armed forces and all Ukrainians who are defending their country with great skill, iron will, and profound courage. America and its Allies support their effort to defend their country and protect their fellow citizens and urge Russia to recognize that force will never defeat Ukrainian spirit. We are committed to Ukraine's sovereignty and territorial integrity and will continue to provide Ukraine the support it needs. . . We will also continue to provide humanitarian assistance to those in need and to back the people of Ukraine in their fight for their country through security and economic assistance. The international community is united and determined to hold Putin accountable."

Soon afterwards, Russian forces deliberately attacked innocent civilians, using cluster munition bombs to destroy their homes, schools, hospitals, clinics and committed worse atrocities that are difficult emotionally to even mention here. I stopped watching the news segments about the war in Ukraine. Unbelievable cruelty as they did executions, torture, rapes, forced separations of families, with deportation and adoptions of Ukrainian children to Russian families, and even bombed a dam. Ukraine forces were also guilty of human rights abuses although not to the same extent as the Russians.

While I was truly upset by the Russian armies' atrocities against the Ukrainian people, I was more upset that attention and finances were drawn away from preventing other war crimes and genocides that were also occurring at the same time in the streets of U.S. urban cities, Yemen, Sudan, Ethiopia, Eritrea, Tigray, Myanmar, Congo and previously in countries of Afghanistan, Syria, Rwanda. According to the United Nations there were fifty-five global conflicts. Perhaps, it is best to not to have the "superpowers" involved because their solution is to fight fire with fire, by pouring more weapons into the region killing multitudes of innocent people who had nothing to do with the "leaders"'arguments and decisions to go to "war."

Russia also blocked wheat and other grains such as corn and sunflower exports from Ukraine depriving access to wheat for poor countries and raising food prices in other countries. A temporary deal was made to allow exports through the Black Sea, but Russia reneged in 2024. Ukraine grains are crucial for global food security. (European Union, 2023).

It seemed that with these atrocities Russia was trying to bait the United States and NATO European countries into joining the fighting and risking starting World War III.

Chapter 10: Israel-Hamas War

On October 7, 2023, the militant group Hamas surprise rocket attacked Israel and along with ground troops killed hundreds at a music festival, killed families in their homes and captured 240 hostages of all ages. More than 1,200 Israelis were killed that day. I've purposely left out the description of Hamas as an "Islamic" group because the Arabic meaning of Islam is having internal and external peace (salam) both within your own soul and the world by submission to universal teachings of God (Ali,

1946). These terrorist groups' tactics are not representative of true Muslims or Islam.

After awhile I started to feel numb hearing reports about the Israel-Hamas's war unimaginable atrocities from both sides. What really could be done? Concerned, seeking to decrease my underlying distress causing me difficulty concentrating, after hearing about the escalating global events I decided to ask for Divine guidance. Considering that wars are a global problem, ideally a multicultural advisory approach would be most appropriate. What would wise elders have contributed to our understanding?

CHAPTER 10: ISRAEL-HAMAS WAR

I said a brief prayer then closed my eyes and randomly pulled two cards from the Metu Neter deck.

11-12-23. Please give higher loving guidance and insight into President Biden's role in bringing peace to Israel, Gaza and the region, issuing in world peace for all:

Metu Neter Cards: **Auset tu tchaas / Sebek tem tchaas** (Ancient Khametic).

Auset is the tendency to be indecisive, easily influenced by others and emotions, along with Sebek is erroneous thinking and trying to ease the way through schemes and perceived shortcuts. (Amen, 1990).

Auset also represents the Mother, our ability to receive and give nurturing. Going into a meditative trance, visualizing healing of past history, childhood trauma, receiving healthy nourishment, mother's protection, teaching and guidance. Then actually putting into action providing all of these physical, mental, spiritual and emotional needs to the people.

On October 27, 2023, after a worldwide day of fasting, prayer and penance for peace in the world, Pope Francis invoked the Virgin Mary as Queen of Peace and Mother of Mercy during a prayer vigil for peace at St. Peter's Basilica church. He begged Her to "intercede for our world in danger and turmoil" and "to touch the hearts of those imprisoned by hatred and convert those who fuel and foment conflicts." "Dwelling place of the Holy Spirit, inspire the leaders of nations to seek the paths of peace. Queen of all peoples, reconcile your children, seduced by evil, blinded by power and hate. Mother, Queen of Peace, pour forth into our hearts God's gift of harmony." Pope Francis also prayed for Great Mother's help two years ago to end the fighting in Ukraine.

Geb characteristics are similar to the need to care for both our body's physical health and the health of the situation. The situation, as we all know, is extremely serious and dire not only for the Israel and Gaza region — the whole world. There are more than fifty wars in other countries of same complexion people biologically cousins fighting each other, not caring if their fighting destroys everything — food, farms, water, homes, businesses —

with no community to return to, as those who do survive migrant out.

This is a reckoning long overdue, requiring us to pay attention, looking at our own thoughts and behavior. Our ability to control our emotions and impulses depends on our overall health. Are we getting enough sleep, quiet time, healthy food, truly loving families and safe environments? Are we also exploiting and oppressing others to get what we want?

There are three homeopathic remedies that may be useful for global healing. Staphysagria is for past and current trauma, physical and sexual abuse, and injustices — including from the news media hyping up our fears. Suppressed rage. Muriaticum Acidum is for those caring for people or a loved one who is dying. Ignatia is for grieving losses. (Grandgeorge, 1998). Hopefully, with ongoing healing we are not passing our conscious and unconscious traumas onto the younger generations to inflict upon their children.

Sebek opens the way. Represents how we think. Are we using our education, logical thinking, attention to details for the good of the whole or do we have a desire to ease the way through schemes with false news, old erroneous beliefs, stereotypes and masterful words? If our thinking and motives are wrong, the path towards our goals stays closed. According to this guidance, President Biden does have some ideas of what is the right thing to do, but must not be led astray.

IChing: (Ancient Indus Kush Chinese)

For further guidance, I consulted the IChing. I threw three pennies or IChing coins gently onto a table top. Heads or tails or a combination indicates either a straight line (yang) or a broken line (yin). I did this three times, noting on paper vertically a dash or two dashes paused, then threw the coins another three times to get the upper trigram. Then I used the chart in the back of the IChing books to determine the numbers of the combined six lines that make up the hexagrams. If all of the three coins in a row are the same then I mark a tiny circle at the end of that line to indicate a changing line. A yin line becomes a yang line or the reverse. Therefore, a second hexagram is formed.

Hexagram 41 (line 4) into Hexagram 38

The first hexagram describes the most recent or present basic situation or attitude concerning the question asked. I read the overall meaning of hexagram 41 first. Then I read line 4, which may describe the reasons for the upcoming change, advice for attaining the goal, success or warnings of coming difficulties.

Hexagram 41 Decrease. This guidance cautions us to not be ruled by our emotions, opinions, old beliefs, desires for sensual gratification and therefore selfishness in our decision-making and responses. It is difficult to assess wisdom, truth and spiritual power when we are overcome by feelings. (Amen, 2014).

There are natural up cycles and down cycles of decrease and increase in our personal lives, the countries we live in, as well as globally. A season and a time for everything. Along with the unexpected losses and sorrows, there are learning experiences and opportunities for true freedom and betterment that we wouldn't have otherwise noticed during times of increase. Often, we eventually come through crises wiser, therefore bringing in a better future (O'Brien, 2020).

Line 4: If we correct our own faults, then helpers and friends will come to assist (Amen, 2014).

The United States has had its own genocide and atrocities history while taking indigenous people's land, with continued forced cheap labor for farming and minerals for production, oppression and segregation, classism, continued mass incarceration, police harassment, manufacturing and distributing weapons for domestic violence and foreign wars.

Next I read the overall meaning of hexagram 38. The second hexagram describes what may be the outcome from following or not following the recommendations from Hexagram 41.

Hexagram 38 Opposition is usually a situation between two people who would otherwise be together, but they are now estranged. The guidance supports the separation of the two arguing groups to stay apart from each other in their own countries. An example is given to parents to not stay together "for the sake of the children" because most often the children are harmed more from constant fighting. It is best for the next seven generations to know what efforts for peace and abundance look like, and to experience this stability in their lifetime (Amen, 2014).

Chapter 11: Other Cultures' Wisdom

Curious, I decided to see what other cultures and traditions would do to prevent and resolve wars. So, I asked the same question using Native American, African, Jewish, Muslim and Christian oracle cards. It is amazing how each cultural belief accurately describes the Israel-Gaza war situation.

"Please give higher loving guidance and insight into President Biden's role in bringing peace to Israel, Gaza and the region, issuing in world peace for all:"

Adinkra Cards: Rams Horn: Humility Together with Strength. (Ghanaian).

Similar to the imagery in IChing hexagram 38: Opposition, of a lone ram who has gotten his horns caught in a wire fence, but instead of calming to be able to problem-solve to get free, he stubbornly fights the fence. The Adinkra card symbol is of two rams fighting. Very accurately describes the situation with Prime Minister Netanyahu and the Hamas leader, both of their horns are locked together, blinded with rage, neither one willing to let go. Not even for the sake of their own people that they claim they are determined hell-bent on "protecting." The Rams horns card guidance is "The ram will fight fiercely against an adversary, but submits humbly to slaughter, emphasizing even the strong need to be humble" (McInnis, 2022).

Sacred Path Cards: 13 Coral/Nurturing (Native American)

The Coral concepts are similar to the principles of Auset. However, the focus is on how you nurture your self, then others. Meaning, are you aware of what you really need? Starting with your body do you get enough sleep, do you listen to your body's reaction to the food you eat and abusive substances, the feeling sensations of intuition when you are in situations or events where you would rather not be, how your body feels when you don't take time to exercise to laugh, play, have creative peaceful solitude? We must each learn how to supply nurturing for ourselves, not expect others to do this for us. Not expect others to fill our own inner sense of emptiness.

The natural sea Coral animal reminds us that we all have red blood flowing through our veins, therefore we all are Children of the Earth. Our Earth Mother that we live on is what we first and foremost receive our vital substance from. Coral also reminds us that our Ancestors are still connected to us by blood, have walked the Earth before us and are able to share of their wisdom, Medicine and strength when we allow ourselves to ask, receive and follow their guidance. Together we can heal. By releasing patterns of dysfunction and abuse in families, communities and countries we can then have compassionate, loving, safe environments.

Be willing to be okay with giving care to your self, being open to accepting love and overall nourishment of your mind, body and spirit. Then you are ready to understand the true needs of others. You can share by giving nurturance to others without smothering them, taking away their dignity and pride in being able to provide for themselves. This is what the Palestinians are needing and asking for to be able to provide for themselves with dignity and respect (Sams, 1991).

African-American Tarot Cards:

Past: 7 of Pentacles. Pentacles represent the Earth, nature, and memories. Again, the need to acknowledge what nourishes us from our Earth Mother and the archetype of the Mother, intuition, dreams, memories, and children. The God of Healing from Ghanaian traditions. Protector of newborns in Kenyan culture.

The image on the card is a young man who has a skeleton running alongside him through a stream. On the grass beside the stream is an older man who looks ill or tired lying down, leaning on a rock. The skeleton could represent our unseen past and our ancestors' spirit presence beside us.

Represents making a commitment, self-criticism and honest evaluation of own work. It's important to remain dedicated, have the patience to wait. Then there will be partial gains.

The role model for the 7 of Pentacles card is Henry Ossian Flipper. He was a former slave that during Reconstruction became the first African-American to graduate from the US Military Academy at West Point. As a second lieutenant he served as a Buffalo Soldier civil engineer that paved roads and designed a drainage system to prevent malaria, traveled and spoke Spanish and French. Controversially, as a soldier he assisted with Westward frontier expansion, pushing Native Americans off their land and onto reservations. However, he and other

Buffalo Soldiers were also tasked with keeping white settlers "Boomers" from illegally claiming land in the initial designated Indian territories. His communication skills helped Native Americans get their needs met in the United States and in Mexico.

Flipper's description of his role is similar to the United States's ally involvement in Israel, complicit in helping push the Palestinians off onto infertile lands and making sure that they don't have resources — in order for Israelis to continue to confiscate land. Flipper's other accomplishments are an example of major contributions to the region and the world when we value and allow all people's talents to grow in a safe peaceful environment.

Present: 0 The Fool – Soul. The image on the card is a young adolescent male happily about to unknowingly step off the edge of a cliff because he's not looking where he's going. Youth have a natural innocence, curiosity, with freedom from other's preconceived beliefs and limitations. However, there can also be irresponsibility, being too simplistic, lack of knowledge and confusion (Jamal R, 2007). As adults, we can also be in situations, especially new foreign situations where we really don't know, but think we know, maybe not even care to know, and wanting to take the easy way out — similar to previous Sebek guidance.

Future: 10 of Chalices (Cups). Represents a positive outcome and perfection of the situation, as we go through a phase of rebirth and renewal. Eventually this brings contentment, happiness and restores family harmony. This phase of rebirth and renewal happening now is uncomfortable but necessary.

Spiritually, to help us achieve these goals of a positive outcome, we have the wisdom and spiritual energy of Oshunmare (Rainbow snake in Nigeria) to assist. Oshunmare represents the necessary acceptance of both our feminine and masculine qualities. Life has transitions and cycles such as going from poverty to wealth, from wealth to poverty, from abundant rain to droughts and from drought to fertile crop harvests. This is relevant as the Israel-Gaza region is a desert with people fighting over, instead of sharing perceived "limited resources." Oshunmare is the connection between heaven and earth with the ability to bring rain, healing and protection. Are we, "Ye of little faith?" These esoteric concepts of understanding that nothing stays the same, that we all have the power to help change the situation in a positive direction is understood by a few. As we pull together with natural affinity and sentiment with our souls' purpose we can accomplish much (Jamal R, 2007).

The role rodel for the 10 of Chalice card gives the example of the story of Joseph Cinqué (also known as Sengebe Pieh) who was a successful rice farmer and trader, until he was captured to work in Cuba's sugar plantations. Instead, he led the Armistad ship mutiny revolt in 1839, determined to get back to his native land of Sierra Leone. This gives relevance to the history of the Palestinian-Israeli conflict and to what is a natural reaction of the Palestinian people to want freedom. On the way back to Africa, Cinqué was captured again by another ship and bought to New York. In the end, it was the U.S. Supreme Court that ruled that Cinqué and the other Africans were illegally captured and sold into slavery and thus allowed Cinqué and the other Africans to return to their homelands. Could the United States again have a key role in freeing the Palestinians (and by extension all oppressed people by example)? The Hamas taking of hostages of all different ages and nationalities is symbolic of the international significance. Of course, it would've been better if Hamas hadn't used violence to get the world's attention. It is an awakening for all of us to see.

Chapter 12: Israel and Gaza Religious Beliefs

Since it is a conflict between Israelis and Palestinians, I asked what higher wisdom and action according to their ancient religion traditions needs to be encouraged for the good of all everywhere:

Ninety-Nine Names of Allah: Wazifa Cards (Muslim): #39 Ya Muqit.

Al-Muqit is the Arabic word for God's unlimited ability to provide for each and everything, a trusted reliable source of all substance. Divine protection to feed and nourish to prevent starvation. Besides providing physical nourishment, al-Muqit nourishes our spirit that gives us breath and protects us from death of the physical heart — as well as closing off our inner spiritual heart that has the infinite capacity to feel divine unity, pure love, and knowing. Chanting Ya Muqit along with Ya Shahid (all seeing) evokes the power of knowing that we are being watched over, as is everything, and protected from want. (Meyer, Hyde, Muqaddam & Kahn, 2011. Khan & Hyams, 2022).

Kabbalah 72 Names of God Cards (Jewish): #29 Removing Hatred Resh Yud Yud.

Pulling this card brought tears flowing from my eyes with sobs, especially after reading the meaning of the previous Wazifa card instructing that protection, substance and nourishment be provided to everyone.

As usual, same as I do with my other card decks, I arranged the cards upside-down, in a circle, closed my eyes and feel where the energy is airy light, and then I randomly tugged on a card. If the card is easily released by a light tug, then that's the card I choose. Therefore, I was truly astonished seeing the Removing Hatred card.

Meditation while (chanting Resh Yud Yud): "I need to be painfully honest. I acknowledge every person or group of people that stir up feelings of anger, envy, malice, total disgust, or any combination there of. With the light of this name of God, Resh Yud Yud, I have the power to drop the poisonous negative feelings that exist inside of me!" (Berg, 2004).

This is similar to the important messages given to the people in Rwanda from Catholic school children through visions and apparitions of Mother Mary, during the 12 years before the genocide in Rwanda. Initially the school, church, and other officials didn't believe the children, instead bullied and punished them. However as word got out the children drew crowds of people who witnessed the holy visitations and experienced the overwhelming peace, joy, love and miracles of being healed of sickness and injuries and given whatever they asked for. All Mother Mary asked of them was that they pray with the rosary, confess their sins to themselves, but most importantly love each other, forgive themselves and their neighbors by not holding even a tiny bit of dislike or resentment of others in their hearts.

Later, Mother Mary sadly cried as she warned Rwandans by showing very emotional, horrifying descriptive visions of pools of blood. The genocide happened because some people didn't heed Mother Mary's warnings of what could happen if they did not purge their hearts of malice (Ilibagiza, 2008).

100 Names of God Daily Devotional #84 El-Moshaah The God Who Saves. (Christian Bible).

Isaiah 12:2, "Behold, God is my salvation; I will trust, and not be afraid: for the Lord Jehovah is my strength and my song; he also is [has] become my salvation."(King James's Version). Israel's God set himself apart by identifying himself as the 'God who saves.'

Psalms 68:20. He that is our God is the God of salvation; and unto God the Lord belong the issues from death.

What can be more meaningful to any human anywhere than escaping death?"(Hudson, 2015).

"Our God is the God who saves; from the sovereign lord comes escape from the death."

Christian Palestinian homes and churches were also bombed in Gaza by the Israeli defense forces (IDF). It is significant that both the authors of these Bible referenced books and cards specified "Israel."

John 4:20. If a man say, I loveth God, and hateth his brother, he is a liar: for he that loveth not his brother whom he has seen, how can he loveth God whom he hasn't seen?"

John 4:21. And this commandment have we from him, that he who loveth God loveth his brother also."

Praying the Names of God Cards: Redeemer Ga-al. (Christian Bible).

Isaiah 44:6. Thou saith The LORD the king of Israel and his redeemer of the LORD of hosts; I am the first, and I am the last; and beside me there is no God."

This is what the Lord says — Israel's king and redeemer. The Lord Almighty: I am the first and I am the last; apart from me there is no God.

Prayer: "Lord I know that my Redeemer lives. Thank you for delivering me from eternal death. Amen." (Christian Art Gifts, 2018).

Has Netanyahu been trying to become God? Israel's king and redeemer, and forgotten there is a God greater than himself?

Chapter 13: My Reflections

Now that I've done all these readings, what am I to do with it? Just watch the readings unfold, which could take months and years to get the full meaning? Or could we each help President Biden and other leaders to bring global peace now? The public is already doing protests and demonstrations. Group prayers have proven to be successful in decreasing conflicts and wars, silently bringing ceasefires (McTaggart, 2017). I decided that I would begin by saying all of the above prayers and mantras whenever I heard news about global crises. This was part of my purposeful, determined effort to not be influenced by fear. If we want better, then we have to start with seeing, believing and manifesting other possibilities.

Watching the news and media reports I get an a better understanding of what the spiritual interpretations and predictions are telling us, and what we need to do. So far we've been stumbling along because our leaders didn't seek spiritual consultation earlier before taking any actions. The fact that we used our advanced technologies for killing thousands of innocent people in undeclared wars is heartbreaking. Writing this book it's truly another tough assignment with many nights of interrupted sleep as I pray for peace and try not to be too traumatized staying up-to-date with events. To be honest, I've learned more than I wanted to know, because of course I have my own biases and desires for a positive outcome for everyone. Hopefully siding with what's right, and hopefully you will too — no matter what religion, political party, nationality or tribe. All of our futures are in peril.

For several days I searched and searched my Qurans for the verses stating Muslims are to only engage in wars to defend themselves, because during the Prophet Muhammad's time the Muslims were being persecuted for claiming a new religion. However the Quran has rules against killing innocent civilians and destroying other's livelihoods such as their crops, fruit trees, water, and animals during wars. I thought I remember reading this commentary in the Yusuf Ali version of the Quran. Frustrated because usually just when I'm about to give up trying to find whatever I'm looking for, there it is, but not this time.

Late one evening, my eyes and brain tired of searching I got the idea to Google "Quran not destroying livelihood during war." Success as I found an article and podcast stream, "Protecting the Environment During Armed Conflict: IHL and Islamic Law," on the International Committee of the Red Cross (ICRC) humanitarian law and policy's blog. Here, there was some of what I remembered!

"According to the Islamic world view, everything in this universe is the creation of God, and human beings are entrusted with the responsibility of preserving and protecting it, and contributing to the development of human civilization."

The first caliph Abu Bakr (D. 634CE) instructed his army to not cut down fruit-bearing trees, destroyed buildings, slaughter sheep or camel except for food, not burn or drown palm trees, not loot nor otherwise destroy foodstuffs, farms, livestock and drinking water necessary for civilians' survival and livelihood. This is similar to the guidelines, Rule 10, of the ICRC's 2020 Guidelines on the Protection of the Natural Environment in Armed Conflicts. No use of poisons nor fire as weapons.

But the article didn't have specific Quran verse references. So I followed up on another ICRC publication and gratefully I found a small PDF book: Islamic Law and International Humanitarian Law Proceedings. The authors' sentiments expressed much of my own sentiments and wisdom. The International Committee of the Red Cross (ICRC) role is to be a neutral, impartial and independent organization that provides protection and assistance to victims of armed conflicts around the world. That ICRC has operated for over 150 years and initiated and abides by International Humanitarian Law to protect all people not taking part in conflicts and wars as well as limiting the means and methods used in warfare. These laws and rules are based on common universal values, philosophies and religious principles that ensure everyone has dignity and freedom from suffering in armed conflict regions.

A week later, in a taxi on the back-pocket of the front seat, the driver had a Quran, The Clear Quran by Mustafa Khattab, 2014). I wasn't going to read it, thinking I probably had a copy in hardcover at home, so I continued what I was doing before deciding to go on and search through the Quran chapters that I thought the verses about war might be.

But The Clear Quran is different, it is only has English and has headings with themes of what the upcoming verses are about. Here's what I found:

"Etiquette of Fighting Enemy Combatants. Quran verse 190: Fight in the cause of God "only" against those who wage war against you, but do not exceed the limits. (63).

Commentary 63: Do not exceed the limit refers to Islamic warfare guidelines set by the Prophet Muhammad. In an authentic saying collected by Abu Dawud, he is reported to have instructed the Muslim army to "Depart in the name of God and with His help – following the way of the messenger of God. Do not kill an old man, a child, or a woman. Do not mutilate dead bodies of the enemy. Be gracious and courteous for God loves those who act with grace." The Prophet also says, "Do not wish to meet your enemy in battle but always pray for their well-being. If fighting is a must, then be steadfast." (Mustafa Khattab, 2014)

"Fight in the cause of God those that fight you. (204) but do not transgress limits; for God loves not transgressors. Commentary (204). War is only permissible in self-defense, and under well-defined limits. When undertaken, it must be pushed with vigor, but not relentlessly, but only to restore peace and freedom for the worship of God. In any case strict limits must not be transgressed: women, children, old and infirm men should not be molested nor trees and crops cut down, nor peace withheld when the enemy comes to terms" (Ali, 1946, 2017).

Honestly, I was truly confused hearing that Russia condemned Israel's excessive response to Hamas' attack on October 7, 2023 since Russia has its own continued unnecessary similar war crimes on civilians in Ukraine. I'm also surprised at Russia's support of Palestine as a separate sovereign state, while Russia has invaded and is trying to force annexation of Ukraine in an unprovoked war.

Conversely, I felt excited as I remembered the elder Native American medicine woman's predictions in the book, <u>Phoenix Rising</u> (Rain, 1987). Many of the predictions have come true, each prediction bringing us closer to the time of peace and equality that the Phoenix rising symbolizes. During this recent decade, globally we've all witnessed major upheavals and policy disagreements within governments, civil unrest as inflation increased, people refusing to go to unstable jobs with less and less wages and benefits, not even enough money to afford housing and food, increased terrorism, mass shootings, war resistance, the beginnings of draft evasion as men with their families migrate out rather than fight, the public's discovery of coverups believing the initial media propaganda but then people begin telling the real history and true stories, and recently unfortunately now a frightening risk of nuclear exchange and annihilation.

All of this making us question, "What are we doing?" "What is it that we really want? How come we allow others (mostly men) to destroy our livelihood (ability to secure basic necessities of life) and environment?" Shocking us awake. With the Phoenix rising it is predicted that the people's resolution, will eventually win overall.

Jewish People Believe Similar About Wars

A colleague gave me an article entitled, "Jewish Ideas of Peace and Nonviolence" (My Jewish Learning, 2024). I was astonished to read that in ancient Israel when an important decision for the country was needed the king consulted the high priest who used the Urim V'tumim divination. In the king's presence, the high priest would meditate until connected with divine consciousness then they saw the special Hebrew letters on the breastplate garment's twelve precious stones appear to protrude or light up. The special Hebrew letters are thought to represent the lessons and virtues learned from the twelve tribes of Israel, thus getting the answers of whether to take action or not, and if yes, then how. Some believe the Hebrew letters represented the attributes of the 72 Names of God. Unfortunately the Urim and Tumim breastplate oracle was lost after the destruction of the First Temple. (Choshen, 2018; Encyclopaedia Judaica, 2008; Gniwish, 2019; My Jewish Learning).

The rabbis of Talmud and the ancient Sanhedrin traditional Jewish high court would have been consulted along with the priestly oracle divination Urim v'tumin regarding whether war was absolutely necessary. Although the words shalom (Hebrew) and salaam (Arabic) are often simply translated as "peace," but shalom really means achieving well-being, wholeness, completion, true prosperity of self and community. Some may think of peace as the opposite of war.

"In Judaism, peace is not only the opposite of war , it is an ideal state of affairs. In this sense, peace – perfection – is something that will not be totally achieved until the messianic era. When the Messiah comes, "nation shall not lift a sword against nation, neither shall they learn war anymore" "Isaiah 2:4), but this will be part of a general societal harmony and perfection." (My Jewish Learning).

We are approaching the "messiah" era. As we open our hearts to receive, encouraged by many others around the world, we realize the messiah is already here — within each of us. The predictions in the book, Phoenix Rising, is similar to what people who had near death experiences saw of the future that all the disasters will decrease and cease as we ourselves calm down (Ring, 1984, 2011).

Chapter 14: President Biden's Plea to Israel

On October 19, 2023, President Biden spoke to the American people. Some excerpts from his speech:

"When I was in Israel yesterday, I said [to Prime Minister Netanyahu and members of his cabinet] that when America experienced the hell of 9/11, we felt enraged as well. While we sought and got justice, we made mistakes. So I cautioned the government of Israel not to be blinded by rage."

CHAPTER 14: PRESIDENT BIDEN'S PLEA TO ISRAEL

In November 2023, President Biden gave the following statements: " Tonight, there are innocent people all over the world who hope because of us, who believe in a better life because of us, are desperate not to be forgotten by us, and who are waiting for us.
But time is of the essence. Our goal should not be simply to stop the war for today – it should be to end the war forever, break the cycle of unceasing violence, and build something stronger in Gaza and across the Middle East so that history does not keep repeating itself. This much is clear: a two-state solution is the only way to ensure the long-term security of both Israeli and Palestinian people. Though right now it may seem like that future has never been further away, this crisis has made it more imperative than ever. A

two-state solution – two people living side-by-side with equal measures of freedom, opportunity and dignity – is where the road to peace must lead. Reaching it will take commitments from Israelis and Palestinians, as well as from the United States and our allies and partners. That work must start now.

To that end, United States has proposed basic principles for how to move forward from this crisis, to give the world a foundation on which to build. To start, Gaza must never again be used as a platform for terrorism. There must be no forcible displacement of Palestinians from Gaza, no reoccupation, no siege or blockade, and no reduction in territory. And after this war is over, the voices of Palestinian people and their aspirations must be at the center of post-crisis governance in Gaza.

I have been emphatic with Israel's leaders that extremist violence against Palestinians in the West Bank must stop and that those committing the violence must be held accountable. The United States is prepared to take our own steps, including issuing visa bands against extremist attacking civilians in the West Bank."

Later, at a campaign reception on December 12, 2023, President Biden made the following remarks:

"And folks, folks, look, if you think about it, one of the things that Bibi understands, I think, now – but I'm not sure Ben-Gvir and his War Cabinet do, but we have spoken to several times

– is that Israel's security can rest in the United States, but right now it has more than United States. It has the European Union, it has Europe, it has most of the world supporting it. But they're starting to lose that support by the indiscriminate bombing that takes place.

It was pointed out to me – I'm being very blunt with you all – it was pointed out to me that – by BiBi – that "Well, you carpet-bombed Germany. You dropped the atom bomb. A lot of civilians died."

I said, "Yeah, that's why all these institutions were set up after World War II to see to it that it doesn't happen again – it didn't happen again. Don't make the same mistakes we made at 9/11. There's no reason we had to be in a war in Afghanistan. There's no reason we had to do so many things that we did."

[During the U.S's involvement in the war in Afghanistan 300,000 people were killed including 4,599 American troops].

So, those of you have family back in Israel, you saw what happened when Bibi tried to change the Supreme Court. Thousands of IDF soldiers said, "We're out. We're not going to participate. We're not going to support the military." That wasn't any outside influence. That came from within Israel." (White House.gov).

Freed Israeli Hostage Pleas to President Biden

Amna Nawaz on the PBS NewsHour interviewed 62 years old Aviva Siegel, who was released by Hamas after 51 days but they retained her 64 years old husband Keith as a hostage. It was then 88 days he had been in captivity.

Aviva Siegel: "There needs to be a cease-fire for them to come out and there isn't a ceasefire. I want to ask Biden. I want to make all the leaders of the world to make the world a better world for everybody, for every country, for every mother that has a child, for every grandfather and grandmother that has grandchildren.

I want to say to all the leaders of the world, need to get together and be strong enough to stop wars all over and stop the war with Hamas so that innocent people will be able to live lives like our lives were before. So I want to ask Biden to lead it. Because he is the leader of the world. And to put pressure on Netanyahu to stop the war and bring them home. We need Keith home." (PBS NewsHour, 2024).

The Reality of the History and Consequences of Foreign Countries Pushing for Peace in Israel-Gaza

It took me awhile before I was brave enough to explore the history of the Israelis and Palestinians conflict. I'm not a politician nor historian. Only since I'm an elder have I become interested in the news and world events. Can I trust the news or is it propaganda? The Frontline PBS full documentary, "Netanyahu, America and the Road to War in Gaza," was a start. It presents a fair overview from different perspectives of the mistakes made by previous U.S. presidents, Israeli prime ministers, citizens, Palestinian and Middle East region leaders, and terrorist groups that led to Hamas taking such desperate actions on October 7, 2023.

Not knowing the full history, each attempt to force "a peace agreement" by previous presidents Bill Clinton, Barack Obama, and Donald Trump was immediately followed by violent protests in Israel and Palestine, suicide bombings and air missile exchanges. Eventually the

Palestinians felt hopeless, betrayed, and abandoned by other countries. Each foreign decision made the Palestinian lives worse, therefore what were Israeli and Palestinian leaders to do? So the conflict has continued on.

Threat of World World III

On October 31, 2023 Houthis entered into the war in Gaza by firing missiles and drones into Israel, followed by attacking all ships in the Red Sea heading towards Israel. This is in solidarity with the Palestinians in response to Israel's atrocities in Gaza. Concerned about delays in international commercial shipments and higher costs as ships would have to travel the long way around southern Africa. The U.S. and the

United Kingdom sent military ships into the region. In January 2024, the Houthis attacked a U.S. ship. In retaliation, the U.S. and the United Kingdom attacked Houthis bases in Yemen.

Chapter 15: United Nations' and Other International Organizations' Involvement

United Nations

The United Nations met in a 10th Emergency Special Session to discuss the situation in the Occupied Palestinian Territory, on the protection of civilians and the upholding of legal and the humanitarian obligations in Gaza on October 26, 2023. The goal was to adopt a resolution on the crisis in Gaza calling for an immediate, durable and sustained humanitarian truce leading to a cessation of hostilities. At least a four day break in the fighting for the exchange of hostages and to allow humanitarian aid in. The temporary cease-fire lasted from November 24 to November 30, 2023.

Another emergency special session was called after the six day truce ended when Israel resumed bombing Gaza. Members of the UN met again on December 8, 2023 to draft a resolution. The UN resolution demanded an immediate ceasefire, that all parties comply with obligations under international humanitarian law, notably with regard to protection of civilians, for the immediate and unconditional release of all hostages and ensuring human humanitarian access. Both Palestinian and Israeli civilians were to be protected in accordance with international humanitarian laws. Urgent necessity of ending the suffering of innocent civilians in Gaza with one singular priority – only one – to save lives. The resolution was vetoed by the United States.

Finally, on December 12, 2023 the UN General assembly voted by a large majority two-thirds vote for an immediate humanitarian ceasefire. Again, the United States voted against the resolution as an ally to Israel, along with nine other countries, stating the reason was because the terrorist group Hamas' actions was not named in the resolution as an amendment. The United States stated that Israel has the right to protect itself against Hamas, while the United States hopes to diplomatically convince and negotiate with Israel to reduce "indiscriminate bombing of civilians," and increase humanitarian aid.

Unfortunately, resolutions made by the UN General Assembly, are not legally binding on nations, but does carry immense moral weight and collective global pressure by the UN membership. Israel ignored the resolution.

United States UN ambassador, for the third time vetoed another resolution on February 19, 2024 for an immediate ceasefire, proposing perhaps instead a pause but not a permanent ceasefire or end of the war. Reasoning was that it would interfere with negotiations with Hamas for the release of the Israeli hostages and other negotiations for a two state solution. This veto was in spite of approximately 29,000 Palestinians killed already, many more unaccounted under the rubble, others maimed, injured, starving, their homes destroyed, pushed further and further into southern Gaza into refugee camps that were frequently attacked. Their major hospitals were bombed. For weeks Netanyahu was threatening to send the Israelis soldiers to bomb the last Palestinian holdout of Rafah with Palestinians having no place else to go. Perhaps over the border into Egypt. However, in support of the Palestinians, the Egyptians are keeping the border closed to prevent Israel from exiling Palestinians from their own land. Egypt threatened to sever ties with Israel, perhaps ending their peace agreement.

For most of the month of February 2024, President Biden was insisting that Gaza's citizens be protected and nourished. He also warned that "more evacuating of Palestinians to the south and the bombing of the Gaza Strip has been over the top" and told Israel not to mount an offensive into southern Gaza. "The city of Rafah and its people has to be protected. I've been pushing very hard to get humanitarian assistance into Gaza as lots of innocent people are starving. Can't get aid in without a ceasefire."

President Biden has also been tirelessly trying to help negotiate a deal that would lead to a sustained pause and hostage ceasefire of at least six weeks.

Meanwhile, Israeli citizens continue to protest the war and violence in Gaza, as well as protesters in the rest of the world, declaring that the United States is complicit in war crimes along with Israel by supplying weapons and money.

Human Rights Watch (HRW)

Humanitarian aid agencies and the Human Rights Watch organization are concerned that Israel has been using starvation as a weapon of war in Gaza, which is an abhorrent war crime, and prohibited under the Geneva Convention.

"Parties to a conflict may not provoke [starvation] deliberately or deliberately cause the population to suffer hunger, particularly by depriving it of its sources of food or of supplies. Warring parties are also prohibited from attacking objects indispensable to the survival of the civilian population such as food and medical supplies, agricultural areas, and drinking water Installations. They are obligated to facilitate rapid and unimpeded humanitarian assistance to all civilians in need, and to not deliberately block humanitarian aid or restrict the freedom of movement of humanitarian relief personnel." (Human Rights Watch, 2023).

In each of its four previous wars in Gaza since 2008, Israel maintained the flow of drinking water and electricity into Gaza and opened Israeli crossings for humanitarian delivery. So why now has Israel changed? Israel high ranking Israeli officials allegedly made public statements that they would purposely impose a complete siege on Gaza by making sure there's no electricity, no food, no water, no fuel, no humanitarian aid until the hostages are released and as long as Hamas continues its threats to repeat attacks similar to October 7th. (Human Rights Watch, 2023).

International Court of Justice

On January 2024, South Africa made an emergency appeal application to the International Court of Justice accusing Israel of using war crimes, starvation and genocide as a tool of war, that has killed over ten times as many Palestinian people than Hamas had on October 7th. These are violations of the Genocide Convention. South Africa also pointed out Israel's destruction of Palestinian history as evidence of genocidal intent: Israel bombed all Gaza's universities, schools, libraries, archives, ancient mosques and churches, looted artifacts, and killed cultural historians, professors, journalists and clerics.

International Court of Justice (ICJ) ordered Israel to: 1. Take care to not kill civilians; 2. Allow in humanitarian aid; and 3. Israeli officials to stop the incitement of genocide. Israel ignored all three of the ICJ's orders. In fact, Netanyahu continued with further worse attacks on hospitals, children and women and decreased the amounts of food and humanitarian aid allowed in. They were to report back on February 23, 2024. The ICJ is still waiting for Israel to send a written response so that the ICJ can deliberate and make a decision.

International Criminal Court

Individual leaders Netanyahu and Hama leaders could be convicted of war crimes but the investigations would take a long time.

Pressure from the People of the United States for a Permanent Ceasefire

Since the beginning of the Israeli assaults on Gaza, people of all ages, marched in the streets of major cities. They blocked the entrances to City halls, congressional offices, federal buildings, headquarters of companies manufacturing or supplying weapons to Israel, major newspaper companies, and boycotted businesses with connections to Israel. Veterans for Peace, especially veterans who served in the Afghanistan and Iraq wars pleaded and protested. To the extreme, a U.S airmen set himself on fire in front of the Israeli Embassy in Washington DC. And yet President Biden still did not stop providing money and military aid to Israel.

IChing Hexagram 8 Unity. Going back to the initial IChing reading for who to vote for president, Biden or Sanders, could it be that the IChing guidance hexagram 8 Unity predictions referred to President Biden not only having to unify the United States but also unity between the Israelis' and Palestinians' leaders? To bring the negotiations from decades of stagnation to unity.

Releasing their stubborn locked ram's horns. To also bring Israel and Gaza out of its stagnant standstill, ending the adverse conditions and promoting peace in the region.

Chapter 16: Why Would the United States Continue Vetoing UN Resolutions?

We all want to know: why would the United States continue vetoing UN Resolutions for Israeli-Hama immediate ceasefires? For the third time the United States vetoed the resolutions for a permanent ceasefire. Disappointed and saddened, on February 25, 2024, I decided to use the IChing to inquire why:

IChing Hexagram 30 (lines 1, 3 and 6) into Hexagram 16.

Hexagram 30: Clarity. Success for following through on the UN resolutions demands for a permanent ceasefire depends on increased clarity of perception, and consultation with wise persons who can use their exceptional spiritual and mental abilities to raise all of our consciousness.

In worldly affairs this is a time when a leader whose firm principles and persistent correctness and strong faith brings enlightenment and order to those he leads. Remembering that we are all governed by the greater energies of the universe. He is a good leader but may tend to focus on only one area of expertise. His actions and way of life will become well known as he is a great benefit to society. Opening a path for others to follow.

For survival we have to depend on having water, air, food, shelter, each other and spiritual faith for trust and guidance. Crises and life challenges humble us into accepting that alone we have nothing. Therefore increasing our faith that the situation will improve, and have the best results for everyone. (Chu and Sherrill, 1976; Walker, 1992; Wing, 1982).

Clarity also comes from having enough deep natural healing sleep, rest, healthy food and vitality to have emotional self-regulation, honesty and reasoning that is based on true facts (Amen, 1990). How much sleep, rest, and meditation time does President Biden get when he is always traveling, going to domestic events, campaigning and has to be alert for the next phone call? The Native American guidance from the spiritual consultation done in this book at the beginning of the Israeli Gaza war also recommended Biden get enough sleep, play, and solitude to be able to access his own intuition and wisdom. To nurture himself first before attempting to make major decisions for other people.

Lines 1: This is the beginning of serious planning for how to bring about a permanent ceasefire and bring long lasting peace in the region. There can be confusion at the beginning of any endeavor. Haste makes waste. He does not allow others to pressure him into hurrying into taking irrational action. Nor will he be distracted by other's impressions and happenings around him. Staying focused on his main goal in order to decrease confusion and mistakes. Keeping himself clearheaded, calm, meditative while open to receiving and following through on higher guidance from spirit.

Therefore he is cautiously moving forward energetically and ambitiously with a firm goal in mind, although of course there is uncertainty. Starting to get clarity as he makes progress. He can be counted on to be reverent, loyal, responsible and meticulous and following through on his obligations. There will be modest gains. (Amen, 1990; Chu and Sherrill, 1976; Wing, 1982).

Lines 3: Have to be careful to not try to hold onto the past and the ways that he used to do tasks, although was successful previously. Change is inevitable. A reminder that life has different seasons and cycles of increase and decrease. Accepting the reality of the situation, with inner calmness and deeper understanding. (Amen, 1990; Chu and Sherrill, 1976; Wing, 1982).

"Do not demand an end to one thing or a beginning to another. Accept that what is right comes in its own time." (Walker, 1992).

On March 3, 2024 President Biden and Vice President Harris verbally insisted on an immediate ceasefire for at least six weeks to allow humanitarian aid in. The United States Air Force and

Jordanian Royal Air Force parachute dropped ready to eat meals on the beach. Hoping negotiations in Egypt between Netanyahu and Hamas will lead to a ceasefire and the release of more hostages starting with releasing mostly women and ill elderly men. This however does not provide a solution to the reasons for the decades long Israel-Palestinian conflict. Therefore Biden has been focused on negotiations.

Lines 6: It is his responsibility to penetrate to the source of the trouble in the Israeli-Gaza situation and eradicate it. Calling attention to erroneous goals, procedures and wrong leadership. It is important to use moderation when negotiating with others' conditioned errors in thinking. Then order is obtained (Wing, 1982).

He will need to go on and punish the unlawful leaders that are causing harm, but give amnesty to the innocent followers (Chu and Sherrill, 1976). Inferior attitudes and ideas must be removed before true progress can be made.

Prime Minister Netanyahu is punishing all the people of Gaza for what a few Hamas leaders did on October 7th and with Hamas's similar verbal threat to destroy Israel. He vowed to defy President Biden's demand to not cross President Biden's "red line" and invade Rafah anyway. So what is President Biden going to do to enforce consequences?

Hexagram 16: Enthusiasm is about what's needed to arouse people's enthusiasm for working together. Decisions must take into consideration the well-being of everyone. Spiritual prayers and rituals with music are very important for energetically motivating the people. (Amen, 1990). Have to harmonize socially first by getting to know the traditions, values and popular opinions of these countries' cultures and society. This will help him get the attention, enthusiasm and cooperation of the people. Then he can introduce new ideas and innovations. Otherwise, there will be resentments (Wing, 1982).

Since Hexagram 16 is the second hexagram, we will read each line and see how the guidance applies.

Line 1: Although Biden had a longtime previous harmonious connection with Netanyahu and Israel this doesn't mean he truly has an advantage in being on top of the situation. He has to be humble and be careful not to brag. Continue learning and doing his own inner self-development and improvement while consulting with those wiser than himself (Wing, 1982).

Line 2: Use other creative ways to communicate and influence others such as writing, music and art. Remains steadfast with his good character as strive towards goals that are what's right. Wait for the right time to act (Sherrill and Chu, 1976). President Biden's speeches are wise and persuasive.

Line 3: Tendency to procrastinate too much. (Sherrill and Chu, 1976). Have to be careful not to hesitate too long or there will be remorse. The right moment for approach must be seized at the right time for success (Wilhelm and Baynes, 1950). Perhaps Biden's delay in abruptly stopping the war is him waiting for the right time, stalling while attempting to motivate the leaders' enthusiasm for working together to diplomatically negotiate for a long-term solution that takes into consideration the well-being of everyone. Problem is Israel stalls in sending its negotiation team to Cairo, and when delegates do come withdraws.

Remember, line 3 guidance is similar to the Metu Neter and IChing guidance from the spiritual consultation done on November 11th, 2023 near the beginning of the Israel-Gaza war; President Biden was warned about the tendency to be indecisive, easily influenced by others and emotions, along with erroneous thinking and trying to ease the way through schemes and perceived shortcuts. (Amen, 1990). Has to have the courage to stand up to some very powerful special interests groups and not be influenced.

Line 4: "The advice, guidance, example, and control of a true, dynamic and communicative leader are a fountain from which great results can be achieved and blessings derived. Every age in history developed such persons when they are needed. It should be remembered here that the IChing is designed for superior persons as a guide to self-development. It can, however, reflect and symbolize others who are not striving for the good of humanity. Among those are leaders who are egotistical, factional and selfish. These are equally discernible. All leaders have difficulties at one time or another, and conditions are never smooth for a great leader. In fact, it is the manner in which they overcome impediments that makes for their greatness. Every leader probably waivers on occasion, when difficulties are truly immense. But by being confident he is able to carry out his will, and gather others spontaneously to him. Everybody likes a winner, and depicted here are winners." (Sherrill and Chu, 1976, page 161).

I've written the above line 4 as a direct quote, instead of paraphrasing, not trying to put it in my own words, because it is an accurate description of the leaders involved in the Israeli and Gaza conflict. Biden as the wiser leader, may be able to do what no other U.S. president or other world leaders before him has been able to do. Especially, to challenge a friend but wayward leader Prime Minister Netanyahu and allied country Israel.

Line 5: Chronic crises with little time to solve them. This is very true for President Biden's four years of presidency (Sherrill and Chu, 1976). Under constant pressure.

Line 6: Many mistakes with wasted efforts, but there are some gains when do listen to wise advice and is willing to change. Leaders could be blamed for corruption and demoted from their position (Sherrill and Chu, 1976). This is an election year for both President Biden and Prime Minister Netanyahu with their citizens threatening to vote them out. Can be deluded by too much enthusiasm, by a rude awakening, followed with the right corrections can be advantageous to all. (Wilhelm and Baynes, 1950).

Looking at the situation from the outside, from what we get from the media, it does look like too many mistakes and possible wasted efforts as the people have suffered perhaps beyond repair as Netanyahu and Hamas seem stubbornly locked in their positions of fighting to the end.

The United States and Jordan on March 2, 2024, began air dropping food by parachutes into Northern Gaza. Later the European Union joined them but this doesn't make sense because the U. S. and the European Union are contradictory providing military weapons and money to Israel to continue the bombing while Israel reportedly purposely withholds water and blocks greater amounts of sufficient food from getting in through multiple border crossings. These small amounts of airdropped food creates more problems for the Palestinians' safety as they are injured or killed while desperately rushing to get to the food.

South African International Relations Minister Naledi Pandor stated on March 5th, she wonders why the international community does not do more. "We all know the most important friends of Israel are the United Kingdom, the United States of America and countries in Europe. If those countries which are extremely powerfully militarily could come together and say, 'We see the harm, we see the suffering. We see the denial of food, water and energy. We know that there are over 600 trucks waiting ready to deliver aid to people in need to avoid starvation. 'If they said, 'To do so we are ready to have our troops safely escort all those trucks so that aid is truly provided. I think this will be such a signal of a humanitarian response that merits attention by the world that all of us would then be able to thank those powerful countries for having made a movement for peace and for saving lives."

Biden has been advised by many leaders that he should use his power beyond simply words to insist that Israel stop the siege. He has to use all possible strategies to force Netanyahu to cease immediately breaking international and U. S. laws by stop giving military assistance to Israel.

Finally on March 21, 2024, after three prior vetoes the United States announced it submitted a UN Security Council draft resolution demanding an immediate ceasefire between Israel and Hamas, to allow safe delivery of essential humanitarian aid, and linking the ceasefire to eventual release of all the hostages.

The European Union (EU) also voted unanimously for an immediate humanitarian pause leading to a sustained ceasefire in Gaza, with demands for Netanyahu to prevent further genocide, and immediately open the land border crossings to allow food and other important aid into Gaza. EU agrees with Biden that there has to be a peaceful resolution of the Israel and Gaza conflict with an eventual Palestinian State.

Countries voting at the UN complained that the draft resolution wording is not strong enough and does not really call for an immediate ceasefire, nor addresses the continued Israeli threat for a ground offense and bombing of Rafah, and as occupier the lack of responsibility to protect and care for the people of Gaza, with instead more atrocities with plans for continued occupation. Why the U.S. draft resolution now after six months of war, over 33,000 Palestinians killed, with more dying from starvation, lack of health care and shelter with their homes and cultural institutions destroyed? The UN Security Council impatiently came up with an alternative resolution demanding immediate cease fire and release of the hostages according to international laws.

Israel's UN representative counter argued that Hamas is to blame for the suffering in Gaza by using an inflated number of Palestinian casualties as strategies to achieve its goal to annihilate Israel, and gain the sympathy of the UN. A ceasefire would only allow Hamas to regroup. The border crossings are open to deliver aid but Hamas loots the supplies.

I sympathize with Israel's plight, however, they are not acknowledging that decades of discriminatory occupation, systematic starvation and harassment would not make Palestinians (or anyone) endearing to love, not hate Israel. Or want to readily live in Israel coexisting side-by-side. Especially after more than six months of constant bombardment leaving many orphans without a future or home. How else would Israel expect the remaining barely surviving Palestinians to answer in the polls the Israeli ambassador mentioned at the UN? Also the Israeli ambassador's

CHAPTER 16: WHY WOULD THE UNITED STATES...

declaration that the Palestinian youth were being radicalized and therefore need deradicalization? In all wars anywhere, the "enemy" is always demonized to convince soldiers to fight and to have public support. Anytime you kill and rape parents in front of children and burn down their homes, you create hatred and revenge for generations to come. The more atrocities the more hatred.

The Israeli ambassador is probably referring to the peace polls used for conflict resolution. The peace poll were derived from the First Nations Inuit people's culture, who with wisdom knew that if they went to war, there would be no Inuits. They lose too many men already to hunting accidents. So they came up with their own way of resolving conflicts. Colin Irwin lived with the Inuits for a couple of years and saw the way the Inuit people brought together a mediator and all the people affected by the conflict, no matter what their opinions may be on a continuum of extremes about the situation and how problems could be solved. This was done in person. Colin Irwin designed a similar system but used questionnaires that listed all the options he heard and then had the public anonymously indicate their choices. He then used the results to come to a "consensus." He called this process "public opinion polls" that later became Peace Polls.

Peace polls were successful in stopping years of fighting in Northern Ireland, Sudan, and Bosnia. It was previously tried several times with the Israelis and Palestinians for the Oslo Accords Agreement. Unfortunately, in spite of public consensus Israeli leaders repeatedly over rode their citizens' wishes. This shouldn't be a surprise as 'western' modern way of life is very different than indigenous cultures where we interdependently relied on each other for survival. A consensus didn't mean the higher number of the most popular votes. There was discussion, debates and compromise to select what was best for everyone. Now a days, so called democratic legal laws have no real meaning, as we do whatever we want to do, while taking pleasure in ignoring domestic and international laws.

As an ally to Israel, the United States understands that Israel still has to defend its other borders from terrorists groups such as Hezbollah in northern Lebanon and the Houthis on the Yemen border. In addition, Hamas is still firing rockets daily into Israel. Therefore the United States continues to supply weapons and money to Israel. How does Israel expect to always be protected when Israel keeps making enemies of neighboring countries. Wouldn't Israel's intense fear of annihilation and over defending, annihilate itself? Make its citizens and other Jewish people targets?

Only after it allegedly appeared Israeli forces purposely targeted three World Central Kitchen vehicles killing seven humanitarian workers, did President Biden have a phone conversation with Prime Minister Netanyahu threatening Israel with serious consequences. The United States cannot continue to support Israel with the way Israel is attacking Gaza's innocent people. The exact words of the conversation was kept secret, but Netanyahu immediately rushed to open up the border crossing in northern Gaza to allow in humanitarian aid of food and supplies for the first time after refusing for six months. Israeli also pulled troops and tanks out of southern Gaza. Biden urged Netanyahu to tell Israel's negotiators to accept the hostage deal and ceasefire. Hamas is considering agreeing to a ceasefire with a six weeks pause in the fighting with the exchange of 40 hostages for 700 Palestinian prisoners and to allow the 400 aid trucks in.

But then, on the same day, on April 1, 2024, Israel also attacked the Iranian embassy annex in Syria killing 13 people, without notifying the Biden administration. Of course, Iran vowed retaliation. Therefore escalating the risk of more countries joining in the war with Israel. Iran waited a week before along with support from Iraq, Lebanon, Yemen and Syria showered Israel's night sky with over 300 drones, ballistic and cruise missiles. Coordinated air fighter pilots from the United States, United Kingdom, France and Jordan intercepted the airstrikes thus preventing major civilian casualties and escalation of a regional war. Israel feels pressured to respond accordingly. However, although the U.S. supports Israel and condemns Iran, Biden warned Israel that if Israel provokes another attack from Iran, then Israel is on its own, without the U.S military to defend its airspace. The U.S. is not interested in joining a war or escalating tensions in the Middle East. Biden pushed for a diplomatic response to Iran's attack on Israel. The UN Security Council called an emergency session with mostly ambassadors from the EU and G7 agreeing with the U.S in condemning Iran.

Suspense of what Israel and Iran will do next distracts from negotiations for release of the hostages and Israel's planned assault on Rafah. Hamas wants a permanent ceasefire.

Refugees from Gaza and the West Bank fleeing into neighboring countries and border fights with Lebanon, Jordan, Egypt and Saudi Arabia also increase tensions on prior peace treaties with Israel.

For months, the U.S., UN, UK, the Hague and Arab countries were trying to mediate an agreement between Israel and Hamas. In the seventh month of the war, negotiators and diplomats from Qatar, Jordan, Saudia Arabia, U.S. and U.K. met in Cairo Egypt to pressure Israel to halt or stop the war and urging Hamas to accept a concession from Israel for a forty day truce if agree to the release of thousands of Palestinian prisoners in exchange for the release of some Israeli hostages. We rarely hear in the media what are Hamas's reasons for holding off a deal and the continued fighting. Secretary of State Antony Blinken announced the deal on April 29th was extremely generous. Hamas' spokesperson Osama Hamdar stated "Stopping the attacks against Palestinians is not generous. The attack itself is a crime, you can't claim it's a generous action from the Israeli side. It's clear Israel doesn't want a ceasefire." Hamas has been requesting a permanent ceasefire and an end of Israeli occupation. Netanyahu vows to invade Rafah regardless of whether Hamas agrees to the deal or not. Hopefully, Netanyahu is only threatening to invade Rafah for political reasons as other Israeli government ministers fear the government will collapse if Israel agrees to the terms of the truce.

President Biden finally announced on May 7, 2024 that the US will stop the shipment of 3,500 two ton bombs and artillery to Israel, if Netanyahu is still insisting on a military invasion of the city of Rafah in Gaza. The US will not be supplying more weapons that have been historically used to kill innocent civilians in largely populated areas. Some Republicans oppose Biden's decision stating that further delays in shipments would leave Israel vulnerable to enemies on its borders and might jeopardize ceasefire negotiations. President Biden explained that, the US is going to continue to make sure Israel is secure in terms of the Iron Dome and their ability to respond to attacks that came out of the Middle East recently so that Israel is able to defend itself but not for a major assault on Rafah.

There was added pressure on Biden as across the United States, college and university students protested and set up tent encampments for weeks prior, demanding an end to the US sending weapons to Israel, immediate release of the hostages and for the schools to divest financially from Israel. Classes and graduation ceremonies were postponed and there were clashes with the police.

Meanwhile, Israel increased its attacks on Rafah, then forced evacuations of thousands of Palestinians, surrounded the city with army tanks and cut off humanitarian and access to water and medical care. The UN General Assembly called an emergency special session concerning the crisis in Gaza. Now thirteen years after Palestine applied for full membership in the UN as a State, and applied again in April 2024, a majority of the UN countries voted for Palestine's status to be increased to Observer State status. This gives recognition of Palestine and its right to independent self-determination. However, as without full membership Palestine would not be able to vote at the UN, although can put forth proposals and amendments.

The United States again vetoed Palestinian's request for UN memberships as the US has done with all previous resolutions. This is confusing since Biden and Congress kept saying that two separate independent states of Palestine and Israel was the only solution. Perhaps the US is worried about the timing of recognizing Palestine as a free country, in regards to the tense fragile diplomatic negotiations. Last week, Hama agreed to a ceasefire but Netanyahu defiantly announced Israel would go forward with the ground operations assault on Gaza anyway. None of this is understandable since the hostages haven't been released yet. With the IDF's soldiers' indiscriminate bombing and shooting, will the hostages come home alive?

UN ambassador from the US explained some of why the US veto. "Our vote does not reflect opposition to a

Palestinian statehood: we have been very clear that we support it and seek to advance it meaningfully. Instead it is an acknowledgement that statehood will only come from a process that involves direct negotiations between the parties." Further, passing the resolution still doesn't give Palestine full membership rights and doesn't take effect until September 2024.

Other countries such as Switzerland abstained from voting explaining that a ceasefire first for the safety of the civilians and hostages is most important. Otherwise, is eminent effective action not getting too late to prevent the extinction of the people living in Gaza and the West Bank. The problem with all of the UN resolutions is Israel has ignored all the decisions and international laws. A very enraged Israeli representative Gilad Erdan accused the UN of violating the UN Charter that was designed after the second world war holocaust killing of millions of Jewish people to insure that genocide never happens again. He called all Palestinians 'a Nazi terrorists regime.'

Again, remember the IChing spiritual guidance consultation warned President Biden and other leaders; 'He will need to go on and punish the unlawful leaders that are causing harm, but give amnesty to the innocent followers' (Chu and Sherrill, 1976). Israel is punishing all the people of Gaza for what a few Hamas leaders did on October 7th. Hamas's similar verbal threat to destroy Israel would be doing the same. The difference is Israel has blindly killed more than 35,000 innocent defenseless Palestinians and humanitarian aid workers. No Iron Dome over Gaza.

'Inferior attitudes and ideas must be removed before true progress can be made.' Perhaps this is why the US again vetoed the UN resolutions hoping for the Israelis and other leaders will come to the table with a true rational diplomatic solution for lasting permanent peace in the region. But has Biden with other countries waited too late?

'Line 3: Tendency to procrastinate too much. (Sherrill and Chu, 1976). Have to be careful not to hesitate too long or there will be remorse. The right moment for approach must be seized at the right time for success (Wilhelm and Baynes, 1950).'

Note: From a YouTube video, I received validation and understanding of my own subtle uncomfortable intuitive guidance in attempting to interpret the IChing readings for how it applies to the question of why the Biden administration would keep vetoing UN resolutions for a permanent ceasefire in Gaza. And Netanyahu stubbornly pressing onward. Usually I don't bother with astrologers' predictions on the Internet because there is enough public fear, fake news and conspiracy theories already. But I was curious about what the different countries' astrology natal charts tell us about each country's purposes and challenges. Vedic astrology can be more accurate than western horoscopes. Check it out for yourself, as by now your own uneasy intuitive interpretation may be similar. An explanation for some of the causes and consequences of Israel's and the United State's decisions and actions (AstroAstrologer, 2024).

Chapter 17: Congressional Pressure

Although Senator Bernard (Bernie) Sanders did not become president he continues actively advocating for humanitarian causes important to the American people such as living wages, fairer taxation, universal healthcare, and no student loan debt. He's on several senate committees: finance; health, education, chairman of labor and pensions; budget, energy and natural resources; environment and public works; and veterans' affairs. He also has been persistent in getting Congress to take action on providing humanitarian aid and stopping the war and genocidal atrocities in Gaza and Israel. Referring back to Chapter 1, I initially wondered what IChing hexagram 7: The Army had to do with Senator Bernie Sanders. Here, as we observe current events, we get an answer.

Senator Bernie Sanders again in March 2024 said to Congress, "It is time to say NO to Netanyahu's war machine." "Let me share with you what some of our leading officials have said about the war and the current situation. President Biden has repeatedly called the Israeli bombing, "indiscriminate and called Israel's response in Gaza over the top." President Biden this week said, " there's got to be a ceasefire and we must get more aid into Gaza. He also said, "We're going to insist, insist that Israel facilitate more trucks and more routes to get more and more people the help they need. No excuses because the truth is aid going to Gaza is nowhere nearly enough.

The Vice President (Kamala Harris) also said, "The Israeli government must do more to significantly increase the flow of aid. No excuses. They must open up new border crossings. They must not impose any unnecessary restrictions on the delivery of aid. They must ensure humanitarian personnel sites and convoys are not targeted. Secretary of State Tony Blinken and National security advisor Jake Sullivan have repeatedly emphasized these points to the Israelis. Pushing and urging them to be more targeted to protect civilian life and to let food and water into Gaza so that children do not starve. You got the President. You got the Vice President. You got the Secretary of State. You got the National Security Advisor saying over and over again Israel must change its policies. And in the mist of all of that how has Israeli Prime Minister Netanyahu responded to those requests and those comments? Here the American government is saying one thing. How has Netanyahu responded? Well, his response has not been complicated. He has ignored them.

And yet Congress pretends as if we are powerless to stop it. Well, Madam President, this is not a natural catastrophe. This is a man – made catastrophe and if we had the political will and if we had the courage to stand up to some very powerful special interests, yes we could stop it. We could stop the destruction and we could make sure that these kids do not starve to death. But doing so well required that the U.S government and members of Congress have to courage to stand up to Netanyahu and to use the incredible leverage that we have over the Israeli government to secure a fundamental change in their disastrous policies. Of course we have the leverage! We are funding the war! And if that's not enough leverage, I don't know what leverage is. . .

But the truth is, there is no substitute for sustained ground deliveries and many many hundreds of trucks every single day getting into Gaza. Right now we have an incredible situation where a U.S. ally is using U.S.' weapons and equipment to block the deliveries of U.S. humanitarian aid. We're funding them to stop us from doing what we want to do. And if that's not crazy, I don't know what it is! Madam President it is far far past time for us to stop asking Israel to do the right thing. And start telling Israel what must happen if they want the support of US taxpayers. Israel must open the borders and allow the UN to deliver supplies in sufficient quantities. The US government should make it clear that failure to open up access immediately and feed the starving people will result in the Netanyahu government not getting another penny of U.S. taxpayer military aid.

And Madam President, I hope very much that there will be a new leadership that will merge on both sides within Israel and within the Palestinian community to make that happen and to achieve a meaningful peace process. But one thing is very clear, is given that the unprecedented humanitarian disaster that is occurring in Gaza right now the United States must end its complicity."

Senate Majority Leader Charles (Chuck) Schumer, the most senior and only Jewish senator in Congress, gave a very powerful speech on March 14, 2024. Here are some excerpts of his direct quotes:

"We should not let the complexities of this conflict stop us from stating the plain truth, Palestinian civilians do not deserve to suffer for the sins of Hamas. And Israel has the moral obligation to do better. The United States has the obligation to do better. I believe the United States must provide robust humanitarian aid to Gaza and pressure the Israelis to let more of it get through to the people who need it. Jewish people throughout the centuries have emphasized with those who are oppressed because we have known so much of that ourselves. As the Torah teaches us every human life lost, whether it is Israelis or Palestinians is a tragedy. As the scriptures say quote, 'destroys an entire world.' What horrifies so many Jews, especially is our sense that Israel is falling short of upholding these distinctly Jewish values that we hold so dear. We must be better than our enemies lest we become them. Israel has a fundamental right to defend itself but as I've said from the beginning of this war, how Israel exercises that right matters. Israel must prioritize the protection of civilian casualties when identifying military targets. I've repeatedly called upon the Israeli government to do so. But it also must be said that Israel is by no means the only one responsible for the immense civilian toll. To blame Israel for the deaths of Palestinians is unfair, one-sided and deliberately manipulative and it ignores Hamas' role in this conflict.

Hamas has knowingly invited immense civilian toll during this war. Their goal on October 7th was to provoke a tough response from Israel by killing as many Israelis as possible in the most vicious manner possible by raping women, executing babies, desecrating bodies, brutalizing whole communities. Since then Hamas has heartlessly hidden among their fellow Palestinians, turning hospitals into command centers and refugee camps into missile launching sites. It is well documented that Hamas soldiers used innocent Gazens as human shields. The leaders of Hamas, many of whom live luxury lives far away from the poverty of Gaza. They do not care one iota about Palestinians for whom they claim they fight.

It bothers me deeply that most media outlets covering this war and many protesters opposing it placed the blame for civilian casualties entirely on Israel. All too often in the media and in protests it is never noted that Hamas has gone to great lengths to make themselves inseparable from the civilian population of Gaza by using Palestinians as human shields. Too many news agencies, television stations and newspapers give Hamas a pass by hardly ever discovering the shameful practice of that is central to their fighting strategies and this has led inaccurate perception of the harsh realities of this war. I believe stories that justify loss of Palestinian life should also note how Hamas uses civilians as human shields. And I believe that protesters that justifiably decries the loss of innocent Palestinian women, men and children should also denounce Hamas for their central role in the bloodshed. When protesters decry the loss of Palestinian life but never condemn differently of Israeli lives, it confounds and deeply troubles the vast majority of Jewish Americans alike who support the State of Israel.

Hamas has been given a deal already. They should say, 'Yes.' My heart also breaks for so many civilians lives in Gaza. Israeli war campaigns has killed so many innocent Palestinians. I know my fellow Jewish Americans feel the same anguish.

And the United States should use all of its powers to influence and bring them to the table and make them cooperate constructively. If my speaking out today has any effect, it will probably have greater influence on the Israeli and Jewish side of things.

But if this conflict is to be resolved, we need comparable and responsible Palestinian and Arab leaders to also speak responsively to their people about the path forward to peace. Now is the time for courageous leadership. After Israelis and Palestinians have experienced so much horror and loss of life, to not have something meaningful come out of this war would be doubly tragic. History will look back on what we do here. Are we prepared together to have the courage to make an all out push to bring about peace once and for all. To bring to this conflict what Dr. Martin Luther King Jr. called, 'the furious urgency of now to end the cycles of tragedies and of pain.'

I've always said when horrific things happen, some turn inward and let their grief consume them while others light a candle and turn their grief into power. They are able to see hope in the darkness. In scripture we read about how God created the world from an infinite void, that out of the greatest darkness can come the greatest light. I hope and pray that from the brutal slaying of Israelis by Hamas and the hallowing civilian toll in Gaza that a two state solution where Jews and Palestinians can live in peace will prevail. I know that I am not alone in this prayer.

There are right now Palestinians in Gaza some of whom are still pulling dead family members from the rubble who are defying Hamas and their murderous ideology and calling for a pathway to peace. There are right now some families of the victims of October 7th in Israel who have been calling for peace, asking their government to transcend the cycle of bloodshed and revenge. If they can find in their hearts a path to peace than surely we can also. From the ashes may we light the candles that lead to a better future for all."

There is much more important points, histories, explanations and recommendations that Senator Majority Leader Schumer made in his approximately 45 minute speech. Several live coverage YouTube videos are available to hear the whole speech for yourself. What stood out for me is the possibility of people being willing to end the cycle of wars and "transcend," doing whatever is needed to live in peace with each other.

I hope President Biden listens and follows his own wisdom given in his speech on August 16, 2021 and take the same stance with Israel that he did with Afghanistan. "Our mission in Afghanistan was never supposed to be nation building. It was never supposed to be creating a unified, centralized democracy. . . We gave them every chance to determine their own future. What we could not provide for them was the will to fight for that future. . . If the political leaders of Afghanistan were unable to come together for the good of their people. Unable to negotiate for the future of their country when the chips were down, they would never have done it while U.S. troops remained in Afghanistan bearing the brunt of the fighting for them. We will continue to support the Afghan people. We will lead with our diplomacy, our international influence and our humanitarian aid. We'll continue to push for a regional diplomacy and engagement to prevent violence and instability. . . I have been clear that human rights must be the center of our foreign policy, not the periphery. But the way to do it is not through endless military deployment; it's with our diplomacy, our economic tools and rallying the world to join us."

Why has Biden not insisted on the same policy for Israel instead of supplying weapons, military intelligence, technologies and training to Israel. Especially when he saw U. S. military assistance was contributing to the escalation of civilian casualties. Has not Israel and Palestinians gotten tired of almost a century of wars?

My hope is similar to the Native American elder prediction that we all simply put down all of our weapons and refuse to fight anyone.

Chapter 18: True Faith and Love

As more and more people are surviving near death experiences (NDE's), I often wonder if there are thousands of people in the Israel-Gaza region and other countries in war zones who have experienced meeting the spirits of their "deceased" loved ones, as well as feel an incredible energy of love, peace, and acceptance. Imagine a life review where you see and feel the wrongs you've done that hurt other people and everyone connected to them. You also see and feel the ripple effects of even your smallest acts of kindness.

You get a glimpse of the purpose and knowledge of the universe and why you aren't finished with your part in it. Most importantly, you realize that wars don't make sense since no human has the power to decide whether someone lives or dies. Ask anyone who attempted suicide but was told they had to come back. Or others whose physical body was so damaged that doctors are shaking their heads as to why the person could ever be alive!

Besides that, wars don't solve problems. Like waking up from a drunken stupor, the problems are still there, actually made ten times worse. There are other major wars and conflicts in Myanmar, Sudan, Mali, Burkina Faso, Haiti, Armenia, Azerbaijan, Ethiopia, Tigre and more countries. All fighting over access to the sea, water, fertile land, safe areas away from forest fires, hurricanes, mudslides, droughts and floods. So called natural disasters that humans cause but ignore the urgency to correct. People are also tired of oppression, occupations, corrupt governments and slave labor (International Crisis Group).

Hearts are changed as those who have had NDE's return to Earth life to make peace and love a priority. For those who have not had a near death experience, but have loved ones who passed over as a result of wars or disasters, they too are being unconsciously and consciously guided by spirit messages towards a better quality of life by spreading peace.

While I was looking for updates on the progress of another possible ceasefire declaration, I was led to the YouTube video, "World is Looking for This Answer! "What Makes Palestinians' Faith So Strong?" (Towards Eternity, 2023).This video has a very powerful message that shook my worldview to my core, as I internally trembled. So much so I was concerned that I wouldn't be able to function and socialize when I would go to work later that day. Gratefully, I was okay after I arrived. Previously I noticed I had eased up on praying so frequently for Israel and the Palestinian people and other war zones. I felt guilty. But then it occurred to me that the Palestinian people after months of bombings, starvation and no safe shelter, pray and spiritually protect themselves. They are not helpless. Have we really considered what the people of Gaza want? Throughout this recent war the media rarely ever gave voice to what the Palestinians, even Hamas want for a new government. They are mostly shown as people who are suffering.

Food and sleep deprivation would definitely put them in a tremendously mystical space and time. The nirvana that the rest of us fleetingly attempt to attain on purpose by fasting and self-isolation or group rituals. I thought about the after effects of near death experiences and increased spiritual communications. I wondered what mystical experiences Palestinians were having.

The video gives a description, "Allah sends down into their hearts an incredible sense of peace and calmness which are humanly impossible to have. There is a divine intervention." (Towards Eternity, 2023).

This reminds me of the of the incredible love, peace and acceptance described by people who have had a near death experience. Temporary died and returned to tell us about it. United in paradise with loved ones who died before them. Near death experiencers no longer fear death.

"For death is liberation from this limited and temporary world. Paradise is promised for those who are faithful and do good." (Towards Eternity, 2023).

The narrator in the video goes on to explain that the people in Palestine are not in fear at all. They still live in their bombed out homes, go out into the streets with their usual activities and pray in the open. I too, hadn't considered their lack of fear because the media images and stories keep the rest of us afraid with only pity for the people in Gaza. Our fears displaced onto them.

"For them death is liberation. There is no death for those who die in the path of Allah. We cannot call them dead. They are martyrs and martyrdom is the highest rank they can achieve in the afterlife." (Towards Eternity, 2023).

I believe Netanyahu has lost his own faith that God will provide and faith that the universe has more power than he. When people have lost their fear of death, how can he claim to be able to attain "victory?" Even the hostages, if they are still alive, will have changed.

Remember in the front of the Bible is the New Testament written in Hebrew from the Jewish faith. Its verses are similar to the Quran and what keeps the Palestinian people strong in their faith and not fearful. Here again is the guidance for leaders from Bible verses in the book, 100 Names of God Daily Devotional #84 El-Moshaah The God Who Saves. (Hudson, 2015).

Isaiah 12:2, "Behold, God is my salvation; I will trust, and not be afraid: for the Lord Jehovah is my strength and my song; he also is [has] become my salvation."(King James's Version). Israel's God set himself apart by identifying himself as the "God who saves."

Psalms 68:20. He that is our God is the God of salvation; and unto God the Lord belong the issues from death."

Notice again "Israel's God."

"There is no punishment in this world that is appropriate for those huge cruel crimes. Just imagine what kind of worldly punishment could possibly match the crimes of the Israeli soldiers who killed and caused pain to thousands of innocents?" (Towards Eternity, 2023).

I've read in both the Bible and the Quran stories of hell and Judgment Day. Some people who have had near death experiences describe hell as worse than burning in hell fires forever. They tell terrifying stories of that being in hell meant being in the same space with similar type of cruel, mean, selfish people as themselves. On their judgment day, they are made to feel the same pain that they had inflicted on others.

Initially, I was unsure of why the concept of martyrdom bothered me. My understanding of being a martyr was the example of a mother who sacrifices for her children, or worse stays in a domestic violence situation, or as true of many women conditioned to automatically ignore her own needs for others and this seen as a virtue. Blames her, yet benefits from her toils. So I researched the dictionary definition of martyr: people who are tortured and killed because of their religious beliefs or commitment to a cause. This is definitely true for

CHAPTER 18: TRUE FAITH AND LOVE

what has happened to the Palestinian people.

Only seeing the Palestinian people in Gaza as martyrs bothered me. An answer came as my Kindle spontaneously opened to page 238, in the book, <u>Physicians of the Heart</u>. Some of the paragraphs were highlighted, so I must have read it before, but now I was seeing it in a new light. Especially in regards to the Gaza situation. A few minutes earlier I silently recited the mantra prayers Resh Yud Yud and Ya Muqit for peace and abundance in the region. I had forgotten the other mantra that Ya Muqit is best paired with. Instead my Kindle opened to Ya Muhaimin. Because they share a common root, it is recommended pairing Ya Mu'min and Ya Muhaimin in prayerful recitation for protection and safety in the world." Ya Mu'min meaning is real faith and trust in the universe that is free of all fear, craft and deceit. These are recited in addition to Ya Muqit. Ya Shahid is the mantra I'd forgotten, meaning conscious of "the one who has the power of watching over everything and protects everything from want."

Soft tears as I read for Ya Muhaimin: "The meaning derived from this root is to be secure and safe. An exact physical plane meaning is to put oneself in front of another people to protect them, as the guards in the caravan would do. . ." (Meyer, Hyde, Muqaddam & Kahn 2011).

Where are we, the rest of the world's population, who should have "put ourselves in front of another people to protect them, as the guards in a caravan" would do?

I don't understand why we don't prevent atrocities, by soon as leaders start talking six months or more ahead of time of planning mass killings, coups, and insurrections why we don't muzzle them and put them in straight jackets, dope them up and put them in a padded room same as we do ordinary citizens. Worse has been done to innocent people for simple perceived verbal threats. Why do we let corrupt "leaders" carry out their plans?

Saddened, we want the Palestinians to fight for and have their land returned. Have we hesitated too long? What is left of their old lives for them to return to? Who would want to live on that haunted land and memories? Not even the Israeli "settlers." Or Russians or in any other warlords' conquered territories. Soldiers haunted too, taking the stench and sight of blood and bodies, along with the guilt back home to stunt their families' growth for generations.

This video about Palestinian faith has a message for all of us. "While we on the other hand chase after a limited life and sacrifice the eternal. Who is truly free? Them or us?" (Towards Eternity, 2023).

How much should our lives revolve around acquiring more stuff, status and power? The misery of daily going to work for someone else, a constant reminder that you don't ever have enough stuff, status and power. That you are never enough for whatever reason or another — smart enough, attractive enough, fast enough, strong enough, etc. The "leaders" also live in constant fear that their position, economy or country could be taken away by someone else's ruthlessness or technological advances.

In our hurriedness, we lose faith that there is a better way. Especially as we get sucked back into our daily routines and habits. As long as man is confused, thinking he has to pretend he has to have all the answers, controls, and be the lone hero we will all be lost, repeating the same mistakes. Endlessly starting over again instead of going forward with a better future for all. The three leaders mentioned in this book represent the three religions Christianity, Judaism, and

Islam whose holy scriptures emphasize there is a power and provider and faith much greater than our own. Even for communist leaders, there is much beyond their control.

Good news is we do now have better ways to communicate, information readily available to make better use of resources and education than our grandparents and their parents. We could have public service announcements similar to smoking cessation and don't drink and drive advertisements, but instead show people how to care in their families and communities. Intergenerational healing is possible as we learn from both the wisdom of ancient cultures and the mistakes of our past. The use of divination bridges the gap by providing guidance in introducing new ways of collective responsibility.

Chapter 19 Our Children

Our Future Our Youth

The Auset card (Great Mother, Mother Mary) and the Coral card reminds us to nurture and care for our children. Our children are our future. Yes, OUR children. It does take a whole village, the whole world to raise a child. Instead we are scaring the children making them afraid to grow up. We have neglected them. Our government officials are like bad selfish parents who argue all the time, day and night behind closed doors and out in public. Meanwhile they completely forget about the children. Leaving mothers and children to fend for themselves.

By refusing to give higher wages, family leave and paid maternal care while overworking the mother until her delivery hour, are we really surprised about the higher premature births, stillbirths or of both the mother and baby dying? Most of us are still trying to understand the abortion bans when few babies would want to come into the mess we have made of the world. Fathers are told to announce "that's not my baby" after being told having as much sex as possible makes him a man. Or to understand why television paternity tests daytime shows are decades long popular daytime television dramas. Men are enticed by television ads to take the money that could be brought home to the family, instead is spent on fancy cars, alcohol, drugs, sports, sex, violent video games, and gambling. Alternatively seriously dedicated overworked fathers are rarely home or are eventually worked to death.

Is it okay that we kill our young? As we lobby for more advanced assault rifles and ammunition rounds, then put the guns in adolescent hands to kill their peers. Leave guns unlocked where a child can find it. When a father loses or is denied employment comes home and shoots up his whole family. Or distraught, plans a mass shooting that kills and cripples other fathers' and mothers' children. We send our children off to war to kill other people's innocent children.

Auset is also the inner feminine energy within everyone, in males and females. However for some reason long ago, boys and men were told to deny their ability to feel, to care, to trust their intuition, to have deep intimate connections to people and to the surrounding environment. Numbed, vulnerable to humiliation and abuse from other boys and men, men bring this attitude home to their family.

By not allowing women to care, the children suffer and the cycle continues. Hence the competition and resentment towards women, when it is not women oppressing men. It is men oppressing men. Men won't stand up to other men's exploitation of their labor, over stressing them then offering them expensive addictions for comfort. Worse is telling men they have to constantly fight to defend themselves and sending them off to war.

No one ever wins a war, especially with the atrocities from use of modern warfare weapons such as is used in Ukraine and Gaza. Killing other people doesn't bring one's loved ones back to life in the flesh nor ease the pain. Wars only cause more pain. Without healing, there will be revenge for many generations later. Netanyahu, whose grandparents' generation survived the holocaust, has created another holocaust on other innocent people's children.

We need to restore a healthy balance of yin and yang, bringing forth the yin feminine within, allowing women to lead in establishing order, true peace and safety for everyone. Men are stepping forward too, wanting to have real loving families and become fathers they didn't have.

President Biden's speeches are wise and persuasive (hexagram 16 Enthusiasm) as he is also a humanitarian like Senator Bernie Sanders. As promised, Biden attempted to pass laws for paid parental leave, more family support and higher wages for family caregivers, childcare workers, better staffing at nursing homes along with increased Medicaid funding for those in nursing homes who want to live in their home community, childcare tax credit and school loan debt relief. He cares about children and therefore knows that family support is most important.

Books, Articles and Videos Mentioned in this Book

Here is a list of books, articles and videos that contributed to my ongoing attempts to understand world leadership decisions that affect us all. Check these sources out yourself for your own interpretation and understanding. I purposely did not write this book in a scholarly way, with huge academic words, book quotes and citations. This is because we all have this knowledge and information within us. Media is just one way to share and communicate with each other. I believe there really is no such thing as an expert, it is simply one person sharing their opinion and experiences. The so-called expert may have done the research and statistics to find how many other people might agree. And they had the money and the time to get published. But life is always changing. Meaning what was true two weeks ago, may not be true today. And the authors may live in a completely different situation than yours, and therefore the advice may make no sense for your current life situation. Books are a way to have a long-distance conversation. Often with a stranger. But there is enough commonalities so that we don't feel alone.

African-American Tarot. By Jamal R. (2007). Lo Scarabeo. Torino, Italy.

Ancient Jewish History: The Urim & Thummim. Encyclopaedia Judaica, 2008.

Pope Francis Consecrates War Torn World to Virgin Mary in Eucharistic Prayer Vigil. By Courtney Mares. October 27, 2023. Catholic News Agency. catholicnewsagency.com/news/

Decisions Decisions: Getting Answers to Life's Challenges: Volume 1 Getting Started. By Haneefa Mateen (2023).

Decisions Decisions: Getting Answers to Life's Challenges: Volume 2 Returning. By Haneefa Mateen (2023).

Decisions Decisions: Getting Answers to Life's Challenges: Volume 3 Sidelined. By Haneefa Mateen (2023).

Decisions Decisions: Getting Answers to Life's Challenges: Volume 4 Fulfilling a Destiny. By Haneefa Mateen (2023).

End Cluster Monition Attacks in Ukraine. Human Rights Watch. May 11, 2022. www.hrw.org

Frontline PBS: Netanyahu America and the Road to War in Gaza (full documentary). Video. December 19, 2023.

Full speech: President Biden Delivers the Address to the Nation. ABC News. October 19, 2023. YouTube video.

Guardians of the Soil: Meeting Zimbabwe's Elders. By Chenjerai Hove and Ilija Trojanow (1996). Baobab Books.

Heading Towards Omega: In Search of the Meaning of the

Near-Death-Experience. Kenneth L. Ring, (1984, 2011). Harper.

Henry Ossian Flipper. Www.en.m.wikipedia.org/wiki/Henry_Ossian_Flipper

History and Society: Joseph Cinqué: Sierra Leonean Leader. Britannia.com/biography/Joseph-Cinque

Holistic Tarot: An Integrative Approach to Using Tarot for Personal Growth. By Ben Bell Wen (2015). Berkeley, CA: North Atlantic Books.

Holy Bible: New International Version (NIV). By Zondervan. (1973, 1978, 1984, and 2011). Biblica, Inc.

Humanitarian Law and Policy: Protecting the Environment During Armed Conflict IHL and Islamic Law.

Ahmed Al-Dawoody and Sarah Gale. 6/3/2021.

I Ching: A New Interpretation for Modern Times. By Sam Reifler (1974).

I Ching: The Tao of Drumming. By Michael Drake. (1991). Talking Drum Publications. (paperback). Random House Publishing Group. (e-book).

I Ching Praxis: Forty Years of Practical Insights into the I Ching. By Ra Un Nefer Amen (2014). Khamit Media Trans Visions, Inc.

ICYMI: Joe Biden: The U.S. Won't Back Down from the Challenge of Putin and Hamas. November 18, 2023.

Infographic-Ukraine Grain Exports Explained. European Council and the Council of the European Union. European Union 2023.

International Relations Minister Naledi Pandor Calls for Aid for Gaza. SABC News. YouTube video March 5, 2024.

Is a Two-State Solution for Israel and Palestine Possible? Start Here. Al-Jazeera English. YouTube video March 26, 2024.

It is time to say NO to Netanyahu's war machine. Senator Bernie Sanders. YouTube video March 6, 2024.

Jewish Ideas of Peace and Non-violence. By My Jewish Learning. (Retrieved 2024)

Know Thy Self Adinkra cards. By Dr. Erica M. McInnis. (2022). Nubia Wellness and Healing.

Metu Neter Cards. By Ra Un Nefer Amen (1990). New York, Khamit Corporation.

Metu Neter Vol. 1: The Great Oracle of Tehuti and the Egyptian System of Spiritual Cultivation. By Ra Un Nefer Amen (1990). New York, Khamit Corporation.

Mother's Love from Beyond: A Healing Journey of Grief and Loss: A Memoir. By Haneefa Mateen. (2021).

Our Lady of Kibeho: Mary Speaks to the World from the Heart of Africa. By Immaculee Ilibagiza. (2008). Hay House.

100 Names of God Daily Devotional. By Christopher Hudson. (2015). Rose Publishing.

Oshunmare in the Ifa Religion. By Dr. Asanee Brogan (2022). asanee44.com

PBS NewsHour: Freed Israeli Hostage Pleads with Netanyahu and Biden:

Stop the War and Bring Them Home. YouTube video January 2, 2024.

PBS NewsHour: Senate Majority Leader Schumer Speaks on Two-States Solution for Israelis and Palestinians. YouTube video March 14, 2024.

Phoenix Rising: No-Eye's Vision of the Changes to Come. By Mary Summer Rain. (1987, 1993). Hampton Roads Publishing Company.

Physicians of the Heart: A Sufi View of the Ninety-Nine Names of Allah. By Wali Ali Meyer, Bilal Hyde, Faisal Muqaddam & Shabda Kahn (2011). Sufi International.

Praying the Names of God: Inspirational Scripture Cards to Keep or Share. (2018). Christian Art Gifts. A Box of Blessings Series. (2018). Christian Art Gifts Publishers.

Proceedings Islamic Law and International Humanitarian Law. Ahmed Al-Dawoody, Nedim Begovic, Zehra Alispahic, Mustafa Hasani, Senad Ceman, and MSc Amir Mahic. University of Sarajevo. (2020).

President Biden delivers remarks in Israel. CNBC Television. October 18, 2023. YouTube video.

Remarks by President Biden on the Care Economy. April 9, 2024.

Remarks by President Biden to Mark One Year Since the January 6th Deadly Assault on the U.S. Capitol. January 6, 2022.

Sacred Path Cards: The Discovery of Self through Native Teachings. By Jamie

Sams (1990). New York: HarperCollins Publishers.

Sacred Path Workbook: New Teachings and Tools to Illuminate Your Personal Journey. By Jamie Sams (1991). New York: HarperCollins Publishers.

Senate Majority Leader Chuck Schumer calls for a New Election in Israel Sharply Criticizes Netanyahu. YouTube video March 14, 2024.

Six months of Russian war crimes and devastation in Ukraine. Human rights watch. August 22, 2022. www.hrw.org

Solar Eclipse 2024 Predictions for Israel, USA, India, and Iran: Are You Ready? AstroAstrologer. YouTube video February 12, 2024.

South Africa's Genocide Case Against Israel: The International Court of Justice

Explained. January 26, 2024. Chatham House

Statement from President Joe Biden on Coalition Strikes in Houthi-Controlled Areas in Yemen. January 11, 2024. www.whitehouse.gov

10 Crisis to Watch in 2024. International Crisis Group. www.crisisgroup.org January 1, 2024

The Astrology of I Ching. (1976, 1993). By W. K. Chu and W. A. Sherrill. Penguin Books.

The Encyclopedia of Oklahoma History and Culture: Buffalo Soldiers. okhistory.org/publication/enc

The Harlem River Arrangement: The I Ching Transcripts. By Ra Un Nefer Amen. (1984).

The High Priest Breastplate (Choshen).
By Yehua Altein. (2018?) Chabad.org.

The I Ching or Book of Changes.
By Richard Wilhelm and Cary Baynes.
(1950). Princeton University Press.

The Illustrated I Ching Workbook. R. L.
Wing. (1987). Aquarian Press.

The Power of Eight: Harnessing the
Miraculous Energies of a Small group to
Heal Others, Your Life and the World.
By Lynne McTaggart. (2017).

The Spirit of Homeopathic Medicines:
Essential Insights to 300 Remedies.
By Didier GrandGeorge, M. D. (1998).
North Atlantic Books.

The 99 Beautiful Names of Allah:
Physicians of the Heart Wazifa Card
Set . By Shabda Khan & Hyams, (2022).
Mandala.

The 72 Names of God Meditation Deck. Yehuda Berg. (2004). Kabbalah Publishing.

2022 Country Reports on Human Rights Practices: Ukraine. U.S.Department of State Bureau of Democracy, Human Rights and Labor.

UN General Assembly Votes by a Large Majority for an Immediate Humanitarian Cease-Fire During Emergency Session. Peace and Security (12/12/23).

UN Security Council to vote on US draft resolution on Gaza. DW News. March 22, 2024.

United States v. Donald J. Trump. www.justice.gov/storage/us_v_23_cr_257.pdf

UN's Volker Turk: A Quarter of Humanity is Caught in 55 Global Conflicts. Talk to Al Jazeera. December 22, 2023. UN High Commissioner for human rights. YouTube video

Visionary I Ching Cards: The Book of Changes for Intuitive Decision-Making. Paul O'Brien (2020). Beyond Words.

What Does Islam Actually Mean? Islamfyi (2017).

What were the Urim and Thummim? By Leibel Gniwisch. Chabad.org (Retrieved 2024).

When Impeachment Fails. Caroline Fredrickson and Alan Neff. Brennan Center for Justice. November 30, 2021.

Www.brennancenter.org/our-work-/analysis&opinion/when-impeachment-fails

Www.whitehouse.gov/briefing-room/speeches-remarks/

When You're in a Relationship with a Martyr: How to be Helpful When You're Not Allowed to Help. By Nancy Collier. February 22, 2021. Psychology Today.

Who We Are: Preventing War. Shaping Peace. International Crisis Group. www.crisisgroup.org

World Is Looking For This Answer! "What Makes Palestinians' Faith So Strong?" Towards Eternity. November 27, 2023. YouTube video.

www.gunviolencearchive.org

www.whitehouse.gov

www.congress.gov

www.house.gov

Author's Bio

Haneefa Mateen has a bachelor's degree from the School for International Training's International Studies: World Issues Program. As with other tough assignments given to her by the Universe, she had no idea until almost finished writing this book that she would be combining what she learned twenty years ago there in college with spirituality and degrees in counseling and clinical psychology. The Peace and Conflict: Mediation courses and her travels abroad helped her understand the overall effects of global marginalization of the majority of the world's populations, their resources and land for the benefit of a few. This, of course, is not sustainable.

www.ingramcontent.com/pod-product-compliance
Lightning Source LLC
Chambersburg PA
CBHW031144020426
42333CB00013B/494